BREAKING HOME TIES

A Salvadoran's Journey

by

RICARDO POCASANGRE

con cariño

11-06-2016

Pocasangre

CentAm Publishing
Bellevue, WA

The working titles for this book were:
El Salvador: Remembering and Leaving and
El Salvador: At Home and On the Road.

Publisher's Cataloging-in-Publication Data

Pocasangre, Ricardo.
    Breaking home ties: a Salvadoran's journey / by Ricardo
Pocasangre.
       p. cm.
    Part 1 previously published as: El Salvador: a memory of
home / by J. Ricardo
    Includes bibliographical references (p.187).
    ISBN 0-9724083-0-4
    1. Pocasangre, Ricardo. 2. Political refugees—El
Salvador—Biography. 3. Salvadorans—Mexico—Biography. 4.
Salvadorans—Honduras—Biography. 5. El Salvador—History—1944-
1979. 6. El Salvador—History—1979-1992. I. Title.
    II. Pocasangre, Ricardo. El Salvador.
972.84052—dc21   LCCN: 2003101622

CentAm Publishing   ricardoj_@hotmail.com
P.O. Box 6276
Bellevue, WA 98008

Thanks to Kialynn Glubrecht   Illustration by Jack Rogers

PRINTED IN CANADA

TABLE OF CONTENTS

Preface

As a student at a local community college, learning English as a Second Language and Adult Basic Education, I had many writing assignments. These essays were about my experiences in my country before I came to the United States. I struggled with the necessary English to complete the assignments even though the story in my head, in Spanish, seemed to jump onto the page.

There are two questions I have been asked and I have asked myself. One question is, Why didn't you write the book in Spanish? English is my new language. Many people in the United States at this time are trying to learn the language of their new country. I am too. Also, I am a little afraid of writing in Spanish, because there is a difficult situation in my country and I don't want any problems for my family.

The second question I have been asking myself is, Why don't I wait and make a bigger book and include my experiences after I left El Salvador? Today, the world is moving very fast. There are not many non-fiction books about El Salvador in print. There is a difference between a refugee's struggle and the story of a boy growing to manhood in his own country. The second book has been started

BREAKING HOME TIES

and will be written but, I have been advised to publish this book to see if there is interest in my adventures. Also, if high school and community college students can read something about El Salvador now, they will have a better understanding of their Central American classmates.

Many books influenced me. I read Ted Conover's Coyotes which is about illegal aliens. Beverly Korbrin wrote Eyeopeners! which tells about real people, places, and things. Miss Korbin said there is a need for non-fiction books for young adults today. Of course, I have read everything that I can find about El Salvador. There are some books on the political situation in El Salvador (and the U.S. involvement). I've read some moving religious books also. I know some Salvadoran poets and writers. I wish my work were as beautiful as theirs is.

My publisher asked me, Who is your audience? Who do you hope will read your book? I hope Salvadoran children and grandchildren will read my book. Their parents and grandparents are struggling and working very hard in the United States to survive. These Salvadorans cannot write about their life in our mother country. These brothers and sisters, these contemporaries of mine don't see El Salvador from a church workers eyes, though they know their church. These *paisanos* (countrymen) don't see El Salvador through the eyes of a politician and, yet, we all want future generations to know who we were, because we are different now. Many factors have changed us. Who were we in El Salvador? We must tell our children.

—J. Ricardo, [September 1991, March 1999]

The description of my feelings will probably be the weakest part of this book. You, the reader, will have to put yourself in my place and imagine what you would be feeling.

In the first part of the book, I write about the El Salvador I knew as a child. I wrote this section originally as <u>El Salvador: A Memory of Home</u>.

In the second part of the book, I leave my homeland and try to survive. From the beginning, I thought that I was only going to be away from El Salvador for a year or two. I thought that the war was going to be short—like bad weather for a moment. Later, after the bad weather, we could all go back and we could work and be with our families again

All the while it took place, in the back of my mind I was waiting to return to El Salvador. It didn't happen that way ....

Introduction:
El Salvador, the Country

At this moment in time, Salvadorans in the United States are in exile. Oh, yes, some of us are citizens, some legal residents, but all in exile. Others, the younger ones, were born here. Some have been in the United States for 50 or more years. Because we call ourselves Salvadorans and because El Salvador was in the limelight for 12 years of war, we are very much aware of being from that tiny country. Salvadorans who have left their country feel the pain of exile. We love our home. Sometimes when we see the riches of the United States and the poverty of El Salvador, we're not sure why we love our homeland so much. The people of El Salvador are poor, but there is a richness in that people-in us-that stands out in brilliant color while the rest of the world is just in black and white.

I learned in primary school that the Pipil Indian civilization named this land Cuzcatlan, "Land of Precious Things."

BREAKING HOME TIES

Yolocamba I Ta, a Salvadoran musical group, while in exile, composed this song about these precious things:

"National Homage"

My homeland has lakes and volcanoes,

romantic places,

beaches, villages with noble tradition,

a thousand wonders that attract

tourists and gangsters.

My homeland also has vultures

that bleed the workers and subjugate

many *capesinos*,

serving rich ruffians.

Color, forest, sun, savory coffee,

joyful people, music, and folklore.

Hotels, duty-free zones, and great

wealth taken out of the country.

Get to know my country, it's fabulous,

that beautiful country, El Salvador.

Get to know my country, it's fabulous,

that beautiful country, Guatemala,

Columbia, Paraguay, Haiti,

Latin America.

A Salvadoran's Journey

There is, also, the sophisticated life of the capital, San Salvador, with its discos, cinemas, theatres, nightclubs, fine hotels, and wide variety of restaurants ranging from rustic "typical" spots to elegant supper clubs serving international cuisine. The list could go on and on, but ask a Salvadoran, "What is our most precious thing?" and he or she will probably answer, "The most precious thing that we have is our people."

But what's been happening to El Salvador's people?

-from *El Salvador: A Memory of Home*, 1993

Some of this history I learned in primary school, some since.

El Salvador, with a total area of about 8,260 square miles, is a little smaller than the state of Massachusetts. Tucked in between Honduras to the north and east and Guatemala to the northwest, with the Pacific Ocean forming the boundary to the south, El Salvador is the smallest Central American country in area, though one of the most densely populated countries in the world.

El Salvador is the leading industrial nation of Central America. Acre for acre, El Salvador grows more-and better-coffee, than any nation in the world., due mainly to its rich volcanic soil. Volcanoes have also given El Salvador the

BREAKING HOME TIES

landscape of dramatic beauty described in *Yolocamba I Ta*'s song.

We'll start our history of El Salvador In the mid 1800's where the commercial lands that had been used by peasants to grow food for their own consumption were expropriated by government decree and consolidated into large farms to grow coffee. Export of the coffee has been controlled for many years by the "Fourteen Families," the core of the oligarchy.

In 1930 the Salvadoran Communist Party (PCS) was formed, uniting leaders of many of the local unions of the Regional Federation of Salvadoran Workers (FRTS). Economic conditions were grave. In that same year, on May Day, 80,000 workers and peasants marched into San Salvador demanding minimum wages for farm workers and relief centers for the unemployed. Their march was in vain.

By 1932, the military government refused to allow the seating of opposition candidates who had won in municipal and legislative elections. The PCS responded with a call for simultaneous uprisings in the cities, countryside, and military garrisons. However, three days before the big uprising, opposition leaders were arrested and the march was called off. Tragically, because of a communications breakdown, Salvadoran peasants and farm workers still marched unarmed into the cities as originally planned. As a result, 4,000 peasants were killed and the uprising was crushed.

As a lesson, the army began what came to be known as the *Matanza*, the massacre. Within the first few weeks the army and paramilitary forces killed over 30,000 people! Peasant leaders were hung in their town squares. By the time the Matanza was over, four percent of the population had been killed, the PCS liquidated, the FRTS annihilated, and indigenous culture outlawed by the oligarchy. The weaving of traditional cloth was forbidden, as was the Nahuatl language of the Pipils and performing native music.

Now General Martinez, under oligarchy orders and with the support of the United States government, ruled El Salvador for thirteen years until in 1944 he was forced from power, though the military continued to rule.

In the 1960's, the Christian Democrats formed a new political party to improve conditions for workers and poor people. José Napoleon Duarte was the first member of this party to be elected mayor of San Salvador, the capital city. Duarte was reelected twice, serving from 1964 to 1970. In 1972 Duarte decided to run for president because everyone thought he had the best chance of winning. El Salvador's military leaders also believed that Duarte would win, but when the election was held and the ballots were counted, the government announced that its candidate, Col. Arturo Armando Molina, had won. Duarte and his supporters accused the military of rigging the election. Then, without warning, the government arrested and tortured Duarte and sent him to Venezuela. He lived there until 1979, then returned to El Salvador.

By that time, a council of two military and three civilian leaders made up the government. The two-army officers distrusted the three political leaders, and before long the civilian leaders left the government because they could not make the changes they felt were needed in Salvadoran society. After their departure, the army officers asked members of the Christian Democratic Party, led by Duarte, to join the council.

Conditions in El Salvador had deteriorated in the 1970s, to the point that many religious leaders felt compelled to speak out of behalf of the citizenry. The government, fearing the power of the priesthood in this 85 percent Catholic country, began assassinating those who spoke out.

Duarte's government took over many of El Salvador's largest farms, seized control of the country's banks and foreign trade, then began distributing some of the farmland to poor people. Soon, however, it became clear that this land reform program was not working, as the landowners and the military death squads threatened to kill any peasants who dared to move onto the farmland.

Father Rutillo Grande was the first priest to be assassinated, on March 12, 1977. The poor formed "popular organizations" to work for change, which included coalitions of trade unions, farm worker cooperatives, student groups, and poor residents of marginalized neighborhoods.

Also, in 1977 Oscar Arnulfo Romero became archbishop. At first he defended the coffee growers, the military, and the government. He soon changed his ideas, and became known as "the voice of the voiceless" because he began to speak out for the people who had died or had "been disappeared." "The church is not against the government," he said. "The truth is that the government is against the people and we are with the people." Right-wing forces assassinated Archbishop Romero on March 24, 1980, while celebrating mass.

State repression became brutal. Union leaders, *campesinos*, teachers, church workers, and others disappeared. Leaders of opposition parties were denounced as "Communists" and gunned down. The armed forces fired on demonstrators, killing hundreds. All expression of dissent virtually ended. Then in December of 1980 four U.S. churchwomen were murdered by the National Guard, focusing world attention on El Salvador.

BREAKING HOME TIES

Many incidents have taken place in El Salvador since 1980, but the story that follows-my story-takes place during the years of sadness, danger, and change experienced by my people in El Salvador, which became "A place of beauty among the ashes of war."

FEAR

Those of us who were fortunate to escape to the United States during this period are not very organized in our exile. We look with envy on those Salvadorans who fled to Honduras, Guatemala, or Mexico, who have organized themselves, who returned to El Salvador, and who have become communities with sister cities in the United States. They have banded with others to stand up for their human and civil rights, and they have begun new lives with hopes of economic justice for the future. They are learning to overcome their fears.

During the early war years we Salvadorans came in fear to the United States and are living with the fear or trying to ignore our past, hoping to overcome our fear by denial. We in the US have become equals in each other's eyes. We don't ask each other, "Were you in the military?" "Were you a *muchacho*?" We ask, "Where are you from?" "Where does your family live?"

A Salvadoran's Journey

We are afraid to organize ourselves in the United States. We saw firsthand in El Salvador what organizing led to. If you were a leader, if you spoke out, if you tried to be a courageous example to your children, you were "disappeared."

In El Salvador, we were forced to vote. Now we are afraid to vote in the United States. Well-meaning church groups and non-governmental organizations are helping our brothers and sisters in El Salvador. But we are afraid of the organized part of these organizations. Our names will be put on a list. We will be identified. Will we be asked if we are legal? Will the FBI or the CIA find us and our families back home and tell them we are Communists or anti-government sympathizers? Will our children criticize us, our grandchildren be ashamed of us? Maybe we should just forget about who we were and what happened to us.

Writers, poets, musicians and church workers are feared by Salvadorans. To non-Salvadorans, these people are respected and held in high esteem, but a poet, a writer, or a priest might tell the truth. Salvadorans have lost their lives to the truth.

The truth became something very scary to me. I don't remember being afraid of the truth when I was young. My grandmother, my mother's mother-*Abuelita*-brought me up to tell the truth. Being called a liar, *mentiroso*, was a serious charge. Archbishop Romero told the truth.

9

BREAKING HOME TIES

Manlio Argueta, El Salvador's most esteemed writer, tells the truth. His books are classified as novels, but the terrible things he tells of in these books are true. They are nonfiction.

In writing *this* book, I have been honest, and I've even written about things that I am not so proud of doing. Though it's the truth, I've changed some of the names and I have not revealed my own name. I'm writing with a pen name because I have fear. I'm afraid for my family and friends. The arm of the death squads—the powerful—in El Salvador is long.

To illustrate how our fear is misunderstood in the United States, let me give you an example. At a deportation hearing in 1986, before Salvadorans were given amnesty, a federal judge had been listening to testimony from a young Salvadoran for over four hours.

"Turn off the tape recorders," he said. "We're finished for the day. So, young man, I have a question for you-off the record, of course. If, as you say, members of your family and all of your soccer team have been murdered, why are you afraid to return to your country now?"

My fear is real, yet this story is true. It isn't every Salvadoran's story. It's mine. Why am I telling it? Though I'm afraid for my life, I'm also afraid that the past may be forgotten. I'm afraid our struggles will just be politicized as a footnote in a history book. I'm afraid well-meaning filmmakers may just glamorize our story.

I have fears, yet I want to give a real-life account from an average, ordinary, common person. I want to tell my story to future generations. While I'm still seeing things clearly, I want to write down my adventures.

Part One

1

My Childhood Days

My life as a child was simple. To my knowledge, there were no big problems in my "world," though I always had responsibilities and chores.

I was an orphan. My father died soon after I was born, and my mother died shortly after my younger brother was born. I was five years old at the time I lost my mother. At that time, one of my sisters was sent to be raised by her godparents.

My godparents had asked my grandmother if they could raise me in their home, but before her death my mother had begged my grandmother to keep me with her and raise me. My mother made this request because she, like other Salvadoran mothers, feared that orphaned boys would be taken by wealthier family members and be made into virtual slaves, to be worked hard for no pay and given no education.

My bedroom was in a corner of my grandmother's house. This room was 9 feet by 12 feet, and I shared it with my younger brother. I slept in my own bed, which was a wooden bed frame with a woven string (*cordel*) base tied to the frame by two strong people. On top of that was a *petate*, a thin, straw mattress. A sheet covered me and I had a cotton stuffed pillow.

When I was seven years old my sister Beatriz would come to my room and splash my face with cold water almost every morning to wake me up because at 4 a.m. I had to get up and round up the calves. At the same time,

BREAKING HOME TIES

my friend Cristobal, who was being raised by the owner of the pasture, was calling in the cows because he was in charge of milking them.

Cristobal was the "adopted son" of my Aunt Juana and Santos, her husband. His mother lived in the countryside and was very poor. She was happy to have Cristobal taken care of by Juana and Santos, so he went to live with them when he was very young. Though Cristobal was allowed to finish the second grade at our elementary school in San Luis, by the time he was about eight or nine he was already working full time for my aunt and Santos. He never received pay except for room and board, so he couldn't be call a "hired hand." He was closer to being a slave. I understand now how lucky I was to have been raised by my grandmother.

Cristobal was eight years older than I and we were friends. Cristobal walked about one kilometer east to round up the 35 cows. I walked in the opposite direction to get the calves. There was one calf for each cow. We both brought our animals to a central corral, the cows to a large fenced-in area and the calves to a smaller area near their mothers. It was very noisy then, as the calves called for their mothers and the cows tried to identify themselves to their calves.

First, I would let one calf into the large corral so it could find its mother. The cow would stand still, no matter where she was, and her calf would start suckling. I was there with my steel milk pail, a 4-foot-long piece of rope, and a 2-foot-long stick called a *cejo*. I would quickly tether the cow's back legs to make sure the calf suckled on each tit, and then I took over. I milked two tits at a time and alternated them until the udder was almost empty. I used the cejo to coax the calf away. I always made sure to leave enough milk for the calf, but not too much, as there was the belief, which I do not believe, that the calf could get diarrhea and maybe die from too much milk. As the calf started suckling, I had the full pail of milk in one hand, and with the other hand I untied the rope. I emptied the pail and let the next cow and calf in to start the process all over.

At seven, I milked the "easy" cows. My hands weren't as strong as Cristobal's, so he milked those who needed a lot of strength. I milked the ones who started dripping milk as soon as their calves came up to them. I always saved Manzana, my grandmother's cow, for last. That pail was our milk, and I didn't empty it in with the other pails, but carried it home to my grandmother. Sometimes I teased my grandmother on the walk home by holding the pail by its handle and swinging it above my head in a 360-degree circle. My grandmother, seeing me coming, worried that I didn't have anything in the pail, but, of course, it was full of milk.

My grandmother would have my favorite breakfast waiting for me: day-old tortillas (made crispy over the fire coals) and a bowl of raw milk. I'd tear the tortillas into small pieces, soak them in the milk, and eat this with a spoon.

Next, I gathered my *bolson*—a cloth bag with a string shoulder handle in which I carried my notebooks and school supplies—and started to school. My school was Urbana Mixta, which was only four blocks from my home and consisted of first to sixth grades. My classes started at 7:30 a.m. with a lunch break at 11:00, and then continued from 1:30 to 4 p.m. I was lucky to live in town. Some of the kids brought their lunches because they had to walk an hour or more to get to school and couldn't go home for lunch.

BREAKING HOME TIES

After school I had to go get the young calves after they had spent the day with the cows. Then Cristobal and I separated the mothers from the calves. This was done so the cows would build up a supply of milk. This was my favorite part of the day because I enjoyed running and roping the calves.

By 5 o'clock I was ready to play soccer with my cousins and neighbors. We played from 5 to 6:30, then I went home to eat dinner. I usually ate beans, rice, and a homemade cheese called *cuajada*. After dinner I did my homework. When my homework was finished, I would sit in front of our house and talk with and listen to the wiser adults. Soon it was 8:30 p.m. and I had to go to bed and sleep—until 4 a.m. when Beatriz would come with the cold water and wake me up once more.

2

Saturday Mercado

Saturdays were happy days in our small town of San Luis de la Reina. San Luis is in the northeast *departamento* of San Miguel, which is in the eastern part of El Salvador bordering Honduras.

I particularly remember Saturdays. Our town was quiet and peaceful during the week, but Saturday was always a busy, lively business day, market *(mercado)* day. People from all around came to San Luis on Saturday to buy and sell their goods. Farmers came from the countryside to sell chickens and eggs, cows and cheese, horses, pigs, armadillos, *garrobos* (iguanas), and fresh fish. Other people came from neighboring towns like Carolina, Cuidad Barrios, Sesori, and San Gerardo to sell their goods and produce. From Carolina came cabbages, radishes, onions, melons, red beans, and dried fish, as well as pottery, petates, hammocks, and *matatos* (handmade string bags). Shirts, pants, dresses, sheets, sombreros, coffee beans, and small wild apples came from Cuidad Barrios. Livestock and dairy products were brought from Sesori and San Gerardo. *Mayoristas* (wholesalers) came from as far away as San Salvador to buy cattle, pigs, and chickens, which they would later resell for a good profit in the larger cities.

By five in the morning everyone was getting ready for the big day. Ice cream was being made, water for

BREAKING HOME TIES

refreshments had been put in plastic baggies, cooking was going on frantically in booths, and other people were hanging colorful cloths up as sunshades. Around 6 a.m. it got noisier in the *tiangue*, the livestock holding area, as sellers began arriving with their animals.

Wealthy buyers, who had arrived the night before and slept in rented rooms in the Pension Oriental, the local hotel, woke up refreshed and ready to do business. A variety of trucks—eight-ton Isuzus, Mercedes Benzes, Bedfords, Toyotas, and Nissans—were parked near the marketplace, ready to haul their owners' purchases. Ordinary people from the countryside arrived on horseback or mule back, driving ox carts or even walking.

By noon everybody had finished selling and buying. The people from the countryside had to sell before they could buy. They brought their produce and livestock—but no money. The money had arrived by truck the night before and stayed at the Pensión Oriental. These were the buyers, the ones with the money.

Most Saturdays I helped Juana and Santos in their general store, where they sold clothing, shoes, medicines, housewares, and all the staples for the house and field. I usually finished at about 12:30 or 1:00, so I had the rest of the day free to do as I pleased.

My mother had two brothers, my Uncle Mauricio and my Uncle Vicente. Tio Vicente—Chente was his nickname—had nine children, mostly boys, so I had lots of *primos*, cousins my age to play with. Tio Chente was a road maintenance worker (*trabajador de caminos*) for MOP—*ministerio de obras publicas*. To me he was a born fisherman.

A Salvadoran's Journey

One of my fondest memories of this time was going fishing with Tio Chente and my cousins. We'd leave in the afternoon after the market was dispersed and all the people had vanished. We'd hike into the mountains and arrive at the river at dusk. My uncle would wade right into the water up to his waist. He'd throw the big circle net he was carrying into the water, wait a while, and then quickly pull up the rope that encircled the net, and show us the fish he had caught. Then it was our turn.

Whoever had remained on shore gathered firewood and built a fire. By the time the fish were in the net, the fire was ready so we could cook the fish for dinner.

When it was very dark, Tio Chente showed us a great trick. He threw the net over a rock, knowing the fish liked to gather near the rocks looking for something to eat. After a few minutes, he quickly grabbed the drawstring, netting a big haul. Sometimes he threw dynamite into the water to stun the fish. This was thrilling and we got a lot of fish, but I never thought this method was quite fair to the fish or the environment.

By the time the sky was getting light, even before the sun rose, we were on our way back to San Luis de La Reina with fish to sell.

Some Saturdays my Aunt Juana's husband Santos wanted me to work for him in the morning instead of working in the store. One Friday Santos asked Cristobal and me to corral his calves in a short block area in front of his house to make a small tiangue. At about 10 a.m. the following morning I walked about two kilometers to Santos' properties. My friend and I rounded up about 45 calves and opened the gate. One of us went in front, the other behind, and we walked the little herd back to town.

21

BREAKING HOME TIES

We each knew our jobs: he was in charge of his side and I was in charge of mine.

I enjoyed working with the calves, but I did miss seeing everyone in the mercado this day as I had to stay with the animals all day. The hardest part was trying to keep the calves from running away whenever a truck drove by. It would have been very hard for me if the animals had stampeded, as it would have taken two days to collect them from all over the countryside.

At about 11 o'clock I was holding the animals back with my rope when I looked down at the ground as I noticed a cow moving a pile of manure with her hoof, uncovering something. There in the smelly, brown mass was a wallet! I looked around and saw no one looking, so I walked over and picked up the wallet, manure and all, and put it quickly into my pocket. I continued doing my job, but I was impatient to be by myself so I could see what the wallet contained. The next three hours went by very slowly. I spent the time fantasizing about what might be inside the wallet. I hoped it contained at least fifty *colones* (worth $.25 US at the time).

Finally, at about two o'clock, we returned the unsold calves to their pasture. When we closed the gate, I told Cristobal I had to go to the nearby shaded area of the stream for personal reasons. "Do you want to wait over there for me or do you want to start walking?" I asked, trying to sound calm.

"I'll start walking slowly," he replied.

At the stream I took the wallet out of my pocket. The manure was now dry and the wallet was sticking to my pants. It was shaped like a European wallet. It was about six inches long and three inches wide and had a leather strap around it. When I opened it, I saw paper money. I was excited, but not too excited to be unable to count the money. Three hundred colones!

Unfortunately, identification was in the wallet, too. I recognized the man in picture as a ranch owner from San Gerardo, though I had never met him. I knew I should return the money and the wallet but I just couldn't. I was anxious about what to do with the wallet and ID, but I did find it in the manure. For the moment I put everything back into my pocket and ran to catch up with my friend. At Santos's house we got paid the two colones each we had earned for our nine hours of work. I tried to act very serious and very normal. As always I said, "Thank you, Señor." I also tried not to appear anxious when I parted from Cristobal. I told him I had to go home to do some important things for my grandmother and that I was very hungry. I couldn't resist running the one block to my house, however.

That night I pulled a brick from under my bed and stashed the money. The next morning, very early before anyone else got up, I made a hole in our garden and tossed the wallet and ID in it. I cut a branch from a rose bush and stuck it into the dirt. As the new rose bush grew, I spent my money very slowly. I felt a little guilty about keeping it, but I was young and my excitement about this much money overrode my guilt.

I wonder if the wallet is still in the garden. The rose bush is!

3

Fútbol Gets Political

Sunday afternoons meant *fútbol*. Now this is not the same as the American game of football. *Fútbol* is the Spanish word for soccer. It's the national pastime and passion, not only of El Salvador, but also of most of the world. I myself had been playing fútbol all my life. In fact, my very first pair of shoes was *tacos*, soccer shoes.

We played at home or went to another town to play. The team was made up of family and friends. We had about thirty players that formed two teams, first and second. We called ourselves "*Pandilla Salvage*"—The Wild Gang.

The first team was made up of the best fifteen players. I played left fullback or sweeper. The second team consisted mainly of younger players who, with time and practice and our encouragement, became first-team players.

Some of my cousins played for the Pandilla Salvage first team. Before he left for the US, my cousin, Oscar, played midfield, and sometimes forward. He was very poor and supported himself and my aunt, Mercedes, by working as a trabajado de caminos, like Tio Chente. My second cousin, Conce, was middle class; he didn't work for anybody except his grandfather, my uncle, Mauricio. He played forward very well and was a valued teammate and a good friend. Conce was an excellent student and his family later sent him to private high school in San Miguel. He was such an important part of the team that on Sundays he

BREAKING HOME TIES

would take the bus from San Miguel to San Luis to play with us.

Jorge and I were the closest friends on the first team. He was a forward. We were the informal leaders. I was usually the captain and Jorge my advisor. It was our job to raise money for uniforms, soccer balls, a first aid kit, and so forth. We would hold raffles and sponsor dances on Friday nights. We also scheduled games with other teams, negotiated deposits, and arranged for transportation to out-of-town games.

The deposit idea was an interesting plan. When another team wanted to play our team their president would send a written signed invitation introducing himself and his team. In the letter, he would make an offer of money as a *fiansa*, a deposit. The amount of the fiansa depended on the size of the city and the distance we would have to travel, ranging between 15 and 50 colones. If our team decided to accept the invitation, I would write a formal acceptance, and then after the game was played—whether we won or lost—the host president would hand this fiansa to me in front of all the players.

Transportation to the out-of-town game was by truck, which cost the team anywhere from 75 to 150 colones a trip, depending on the distance. Every player and every fan going with us had to pay part of the fee to be allowed to stand on the truck. I think all the towns had the same arrangement.

But the purpose of the fiansa was not to pay for transportation. Partly it served as insurance that the host team would travel to the visiting team's town for the "return engagement," as they would then get their fianza back. Another reason was to make sure that the host team didn't harass our players or fans.

A Salvadoran's Journey

We had had incidents that made this fianza money very important. One team we played out in the countryside beat rifles and machetes on the ground behind our goal shouting, "Let our team score or we'll use these." Our goalie let one score get by, and then we kept the deposit money and never again invited them to play at our home field.

All the players had responsibilities at the Friday night dances. These obligations were well defined during practice. The most important instruction was to bring your sisters, cousins, aunts—FEMALES—to the dance. If we knew girls who didn't have brothers on the team, a group of us would pick up the girls at their homes and walk them back home after the dance. The girls didn't pay, but the *varones* (males) did, and if there were lots of females, lots of paying guys came.

At one of these dances we had a scary incident. Santana had played defense on the second team before he was forcibly recruited by the government civil defense army. One day he had been walking along the street when soldiers approached him from both sides of the street and picked him up. Because Santana was poor, nobody went to the brigade headquarters to bribe the lieutenant to release him. About three months later he came back to town on a three-day pass. He had a uniform, a hat, and a very short haircut. He showed up at one of the regular Friday night fund-raising dances.

The night Santana first came home on leave, there were about thirty guys standing in line waiting to pay their two colones to get in. He walked up to the front of the line, behind the fourth guy in line, and elbowed his way in.

"Can't you see that everybody who's just arriving goes to the back of the line?" he was told.

BREAKING HOME TIES

Santana replied to the guy in line, "See my uniform? I can do whatever I want." Then, in a loud voice that almost everyone in the town could hear, he said, "Don't you understand that I'm worth ten of you civilians?"

Romero and Mendez were two of our team members. We called them by their last names because we never knew their first names. They weren't originally from San Luis. They were two of the seven National Guardsmen who already had been stationed in our town before this dance. Romero was a midfield player and he was good. Mendez played forward, and he wasn't bad but he wasn't very good either. After about a year of playing on our team there was a switch in commanding officers and the new officer didn't like the name of our team—The Wild Gang—so he ordered Romero and Mendez not to play with us anymore.

We needed to replace these guys, so we moved Victor and Freddy up to play on the first team. Even though they were nearly ten years younger than Jorge and I, Victor and Freddy were our closest friends on the second team, and we were good companions off the field as well. When we were younger Victor, Freddy, Jorge, and I played pool together (when Vic's and Freddy's teachers weren't around), and now all four of us had rather long hair. The European professional soccer players we saw playing on TV had long hair, and I guess they became our role models.

By 1979, about a month after the new National Guard officer arrived, the team was practicing and we noticed that four Guardsmen were walking onto the field. I stopped playing, walked about 15 or 20 yards over to them, and asked, "Can I help you?"

The new officer was one of the four. "Yes, I am here to give you an order." He reached into his shirt pocket, drew

28

out a little note card, and read. "Ricardo, Freddy, Victor, and Jorge have 48 hours to cut your hair like decent people. If you don't and we find any of you with long hair, we'll cut it with a machete." For emphasis, he patted the machete hanging at his side.

"I'm a civilian," I said. "Am I breaking the law?"

"Only Communists have long hair and beards," was his reply.

I just looked him in the eyes, walked away, and continued practicing. Most of the players hadn't heard our conversation because we were just out of hearing range, so when I came back on the field, they bombarded me with questions: "Who are they looking for?" "We saw him pull some paper from his shirt. Did they want one of us?"

"It was for me and another three players," I told them, "but don't worry, we are not going to jail. We are not criminals."

As their captain, they trusted me. They just looked at me and smiled. We went back to practicing.

After the practice I signaled to Victor, Freddy, and Jorge. This incident took place on a Friday afternoon, just before dinner, so everyone else rushed to change out of his shorts and T-shirts into pants and shirts and took off quickly for home.

As soon as Vic, Freddy, Jorge, and I were alone, I told them what had happened, that the officer had given us an order to cut our hair within 48 hours. The guys were furious. Freddy, who had the longest hair, made up his mind not to have his hair cut "like decent people." We came up with an idea. We all agreed to go together to the same barber the following day, Saturday. We decided we'd have our hair cut our way.

BREAKING HOME TIES

Sunday noon, when we walked onto the field the crowd whistled and yelled. They asked each other, "Who are those light-bulb-headed guys? Are they from earth or another planet?"

By the time we had taken our positions on the field, the crowd had recognized us, despite our completely bald heads. But they all wanted to know why we had shaved. Nobody knew why but the National Guard and the four of us. It was very hot that Sunday. At half time the whole team went to stand together under the shade of a tree. Fans—kids and adults alike—came to look closer. One little boy ran his hand over my head and said, " It feels good. It tickles my palm." One person who knew I played left defense commented, "This way you can head the ball farther!"

After the game we went over to where our street clothes were, dressed, and started walking up the little bank from the field. To do this, we had to pass the National Guardsmen, who were standing above us about a block away. I was eating a popsicle and tried to ignore them, but one of the guardsmen yelled, "Hey you, *Pelon,* (Baldie), come here."

I obeyed and he said, "We don't like your haircuts. Only Communists cut their hair that way."

"You told me Communists have long hair and beards," I said, then turned and walked away.

4

I Almost Kill A Man

When I was younger, picking coffee was a fun break from home and school., I had started picking coffee with my uncles and cousins when I was eleven, then as a young adult I picked coffee to buy "extras"—a new pair of tacos, sometimes a T-shirt.

October is the end of the rainy season in El Salvador. Everything looks so green. We have a saying, "Los vientos de Octubre, que todo lo descubre" ("The winds of October discover everything"). We would leave San Luis when the winds started blowing around the end of October, after school was out for the year. As many of us as could fit would pile into my uncle Santos' truck to go to a coffee plantation in the mountains.

There the men and older boys would build a makeshift shack of sticks covered with plastic tarps, where we slept and where we used it for shade from the hot sun. Each year, it took about six weeks for the whole family to pick all the coffee beans at this plantation. The adults would gather all the beans they could reach on the 12-foot coffee bushes while standing on the ground, leaving the beans higher up for the kids. I liked climbing to the top, gathering the beans, and putting them into my tummy bag.

I remember after the coffee season in 1979 my aunt Mercedes moved temporarily to San Salvador, leaving her home and its contents behind. Now at twenty-six, I was in charge of keeping an eye on things as her son had gone to the United States to try to make more money. The house was small, about the size of a large kitchen, with no walls, even to separate the two beds. The floor was hard-packed dirt, except under the beds, where my cousin Oscar, her son, had made a pretty pattern of tiles set into the dirt. Aunt Mercedes had, of course, left most of her clothes, all of her dishes, pots, and pans, and the table and chairs—all the things that go into a very modest Salvadoran home.

I usually went every other day to check on the house. One day I opened the front door with the key. I immediately noticed that the tiles under the beds were nearly all missing and that a couple of big clay water jugs had disappeared. I checked the back door, which was usually fastened by bracing the door from inside with a plank of wood or a log and saw that the plank wasn't as I had left it. It looked as if someone had left through the back door, leaning the plank against the door by wrapping his arm behind the door from the outside.

As I left, I put the plank back into place and closed and locked the door, wondering who was stealing these things from my poor aunt. I asked a friendly neighbor if he had noticed anyone around and he said he hadn't. I guessed the break-in probably had happened during the night, reasoning that the neighbor would have been observant only during the daytime.

That night I went back with a flashlight and a gun, which I had taken from my sister without permission, and locked myself inside the house to surprise the thief. I lay in the hammock between the two beds, waiting and listening in the dark. The night was long and quiet, except for dogs barking, crickets chirping, and frogs croaking, but I didn't close my eyes even for a second, holding the gun ready in one hand and the flashlight in the other. Though I spent the whole night there, I saw no one. I returned home at 6 a.m., had breakfast, and fell asleep in my own bed.

I wondered if there were some other way to find out about the thief, but couldn't think of any alternatives, so I returned to spend yet another night in the dark, again with no thief. However, this time when I returned to my house in the morning, I heard my cousin Anita say to my sister and grandmother in a very upset tone, "Somebody broke into my store and stole a lot of merchandise. He wiped me out. He took money, shoes, cans of food. Everything!" She showed me how the thief had removed tiles from the roof, then squeezed into the store. I thought this might be the same thief who was stealing from my Aunt Mercedes' house.

In the next few days, Anita began to suspect that the thief was Calandria, because his girlfriend started showing up with shirts, shoes, and other things that Anita thought had been stolen from her store. *Calandria* is the Spanish word for lark, and the nickname had been given first to Calandria's father, who was an alcoholic who had died young, so the nickname was passed on to his child. Calandria was younger than I. I always remember him just hanging around our town doing odd jobs while everyone else was away picking coffee. Like Anita, I too suspected Calandria because I had observed that he always had money, even though he never did any work for it, and thought maybe he was selling the things he took from my aunt's store to people around town.

About a week and a half after Anita's store had been broken into, on a Sunday morning about 8 o'clock, I walked very softly and quietly up to my Aunt Mercedes' house and peered through the cracks between the door

BREAKING HOME TIES

jamb. Calandria was asleep in the hammock. I reached in my pocket for the key and unlocked the door as quietly as I could. I pulled the .357 Magnum out of the front waistband of my pants, opened the door with one hand, and pointed my gun in the direction of the hammock. I thought, "People who steal from poor people deserve to be killed!" At that moment I was acting as if I was the law—the judge and the jury.

I saw that Calandria had placed his machete under the hammock and knew that he could have reached it from where he lay, so I was really careful. I put the gun in front of me, held it with two hands, then woke him up.

"Calandria!" I yelled. I was thinking, "Are you ready to go to Hell, Calandria? I am ready to blow your brains out!"

He woke, startled, but didn't grab for his machete, only turned and looked at me in total surprise. I didn't take my eyes from him and held the gun absolutely steady, waiting for one false move.

I told him, "I'm going to kill you not because of what you have taken, but because you have stolen from a poor lady who doesn't have anybody around here."

"I just use the house to sleep," Calandria blurted out. "I haven't stolen anything."

At that moment the neighbor from next door came over and stepped into the doorway. Calandria pleaded for his help. "I don't want to die. I haven't taken anything!"

"I don't believe that," the neighbor said. "You are the only person who has been found inside this house."

The neighbor turned to me, winked, and said, "The decision is in your hands. I know the town will be happy if you do this, but is it worth staining your hands with the blood of that little rat?"

A Salvadoran's Journey

That made me remember that my grandmother had often said to me: "Ricardo, do not kill or stain your hands with blood."

I still had my gun pointed at Calandria. I made him promise never to come near my aunt's house again. I said, "You should be glad I am letting you go. Next time I will shoot you on sight. I will not waste my saliva on giving you a warning."

The neighbor and I watched while Calandria ran out the door. I was a still upset and angry. I felt that a despicable person like he deserved to die, but I was also glad I was not the person who took the life of another human being. The neighbor said, "Don't worry. Calandria will not last long the way he's going."

"I don't know," I said. "Sometimes bad people last longer and good people die young."

As I started away, the neighbor turned and yelled over his shoulder, "Don't turn your back to him!"

It didn't take long before Calandria met his end.

It happened on a Friday night about two weeks after my encounter with him. On Friday nights San Luis de La Reina always had many out-of-town visitors, business people waiting for the Saturday morning's mercardo. A handful of men were playing pool, with at least another thirty hanging around in the poolroom. Varones, *niños* (kids) also, but no females, were walking in and out of the club.

The little club had two pool tables. The major profit for the owner wasn't pool, but gambling—dice. The National Guard had been stationed in our town for many years, living in a barracks. The seven men that had been there since before 1978 were joined by eight more men, so now in 1979 there were fifteen in San Luis. Every weekend the

BREAKING HOME TIES

club's owner bribed the National Guard to permit the gambling, and two or three times a month eight men or so would gamble all night. In the mornings when everyone dispersed there was always a lot of complaining because, of course, the owner always won as he took ten centavos every time a colon (100 centavos) was wagered. Back and forth ten times, and the owner had a colon. In the Saturday morning daylight these men were tired, angry, poor, and without the energy to buy or sell at the market. Most of the time the people of San Luis knew who the men were who were deep into gambling, and a lot of people felt sorry for the "unluckies," though I didn't, because they themselves chose to waste their money this way.

At about 8 o'clock in the evening I was a block away from the poolroom, standing on the balcony of my married sister's home looking towards the pool room, watching the men coming and going into Club San Luis. Two shots rang out. Everyone froze. We saw three men in civilian clothes walk out of the club. When they were in the street, one by one they shot twice in the air. They passed in front of the post office light, then ten yards further down they turned and walked into the darkness. It felt like a very long time before the rest of the people started coming out of the pool room, but it was probably no more than three to five minutes after the first three men had come out.

I ran downstairs and out onto the street. I asked people coming out of the club what had happened. The first person I asked didn't answer. He didn't even look at me, just kept walking. I spotted one of my young friends. "What happened?" I asked him.

He answered reluctantly. "Calandria's dead."

"Who did it?"

A Salvadoran's Journey

He looked me straight in the eyes and said, "I don't know. I was looking in the other direction."

I continued walking towards the club. A few old men stood not too far from the doorway. I said hello to them, then continued walking into the poolroom. The three front doors of the hall were wide open and the lights were on. I passed the first door and walked through the second door. I stepped into the third doorway between the two pool tables. To my left I saw Calandria's body lying under the pool table in a puddle of blood. There wasn't another soul in the place. I stepped back—a little nervous and scared—and walked out.

Outside people had gathered to discuss the shooting. I learned that it had been Calandria's turn to shoot the ball. He was leaning with half of his body over the table and his back to the door when a National Guardsman came from behind. Before Calandria could take his shot, the Guardsman touched Calandria's left shoulder with one hand. When Calandria turned around to see whom it was there was a gun against his temple. The bullet came out the other side of his head. The killer fired again. The second bullet grazed the back of Calandria's neck and struck the pool table.

Some say that the National Guardsmen had become too friendly with some businessmen in San Luis. It might have been that some people in town didn't like Calandria's thieving and asked a Guardsman to "take care of matter." Cold-blooded murder would frighten boys and grown men to look the other way.

Calandria's mother came, crying, and more running than walking, only to find her son dead in a pool of blood. I felt very sad for her and thanked God for having given me the strength to refrain from doing that to another person.

BREAKING HOME TIES

The Justice of the Peace who was supposed to come and identify the body and record the cause of death didn't come until the next morning. Only Calandria's mother stayed with her dead son all night. Calandria's family was poor, and nobody liked him, but his mother wanted to give a proper funeral to her son. The next day a group of people went around asking for contributions to buy a coffin for him. I had ten colones in my wallet. I gladly gave it to them, then joined them to ask others for contributions.

5

The Death Squads Enter Our Lives

Most Sunday mornings at nine, just after breakfast, my family, like many people in El Salvador, heard Monsignor Romero's radio broadcasts from San Salvador. My grandmother, my sister Beatriz, my nephews and nieces, and I sat close to the radio and listened intently. In his sermons, Monsignor Romero would call for a cease-fire to stop the killings taking place all over the country. He'd tell who was missing, who had been disappeared. (To be "disappeared" is a verb that had come into usage since the war in El Salvador began. The meaning is something like "to be kidnapped and never seen again.") Every Sunday Romero begged the army, "Don't obey any orders that go against God's law. Don't kill your brothers!"

Archbishop Romero's March 17 sermon was longer than usual, and he paused many times. We were worried, but decided that it was probably because he was growing increasingly upset because of the rise in violations against the civilian population by the army.

That afternoon when we met on the soccer field, there was a lot of tension. Everyone had heard the broadcast and wondered what was going on. Some players said that Romero didn't have "hairs on his tongue," that he really spoke the truth. (If someone had hairs on his tongue, he wouldn't have the courage to tell the truth.) We were all afraid of what could happen to this brave priest. The archbishop didn't mention names, but I knew from reading some homemade flyers that priests were being murdered all over the country. I didn't discuss all my thoughts with my teammates, but I felt that something was about to shock our country.

Then, a week later, March 24, 1980, we heard a news report that Monsignor Romero had been assassinated during that day's mass.

I was filled with dread. I felt that the situation in the country was going to get worse, and I was deeply saddened and very worried. I was caring for my grandmother, my sister Beatriz, her younger children, the property, and the livestock.

At this time I was still working for Santos at his general store in San Luis. My job was to load and unload 200-pound bags of grain, feed, and other supplies from the store's eight-ton truck. I know the exact weight because it was my job to put 200 pounds of grain into a two-pound hemp sack and sew, not tie, it up.

Twice a week we'd take the loaded truck to San Miguel, the large city 3 1/2 hours away, to sell the grain. While we were there, I usually was able to visit with my close friend Victor, who was Santos' son. His parents had sent him there to live with his older sisters and brother while attending high school. Since our school in San Luis, Urbana Mixta, only went to sixth grade at the time, one had to pay for further education and move to a larger city if you continued school after 6th grade. Victor was studying accounting in *colegio* (equivalent to U.S. secondary school) in San Miguel, hoping to go into business like his father.

Victor and I were careful to not talk about the political situation because had anyone overheard us we would have been in a great deal of trouble.

A Salvadoran's Journey

One weekend when Victor came home to San Luis we went for a walk. He told me about the recent events at this school. He was visibly shaken and grew more upset as he talked.

"Four men carrying military weapons were standing in front of the main door of the colegio. Students and teachers were coming and going through the door. The men seemed to be waiting for somebody specific. As my English teacher came toward the main door, the four men fired at least twice each, and the teacher fell dead on the sidewalk. Everyone scattered to safety. Then four of my classmates ran out of the building and saw our teacher on the ground. The four death-squad members pointed their machine guns at them, ordering my friends to go with them."

As Victor talked, I could hear the sadness in his voice and see the fear in his eyes. He told me that two days later, on the on the road to La Union on the outskirts of San Miguel the four students were found tortured to death.

Victor continued. "Another teacher of mine, who was also a law student at the National University, was taken from his home. They found him later. He had been tortured to death."

Victor spoke slowly, partly so I wouldn't miss anything he had to say and partly because he was so upset. I was the first person he had talked to about these killings.

Victor also told me that a month and a half earlier he had been at a meeting with his school's soccer team. They were all discussing how they could help with agrarian reform. Suddenly they heard a commotion, and about fifty National Guardsmen in uniform drove up in a small car and two trucks. Most of the teammates were able to escape, but the guardsmen captured four of them. Victor ran and hid in the outhouse of a nearby *meson*. (A meson is a group of stuck-together, shack-like houses with one outside entrance and an outhouse in its center courtyard.)

Victor told his story: A guardsman pounded on the door. "Open up or we'll knock the door down." I unlocked the door, still sitting down.

"Come out!"

I stood up and walked out, zipping my pants and buckling my belt.

The guardsman asked, "Where do you live?"

I pointed to one of the shacks in the meson and said, "There. Why?"

The guardsman walked to the door and knocked on it. An older woman opened the door. I held my breath.

"Is this your son?"

"Yes," the woman lied. "What's wrong?"

"Nothing—with him."

Victor walked into the woman's house and they watched while the guardsman joined the rest of the guard outside the front entrance of the meson where the captured four were being held.

Victor's stories had me worried for his safety, but we took him back to school on his father's truck on Monday morning. During the week I heard that a demonstration had taken place in San Salvador, where the army killed fifty students and another twenty-seven had been disappeared.

One week later, June 27, 1980, it was a relief to see Victor again. He told me more gruesome stories about friends, classmates, and teammates being killed. He also told me that the afternoon I had driven him to San Miguel Alex, one of his best friends in San Miguel, had been about to go to soccer practice when the death squads came to his house, about a block and a half from where Victor was walking. He saw Alex shinny up a utility pole and was repeatedly machine gunned as his body slipped down the pole.

"Ricardo, the army death squads have killed my closest friends—eight out of twelve of the guys on my team.

"Rica, I didn't tell you before, but Juan was one of the four taken prisoner at the meson. I saw Juan's body two days later. His eyes had been poked out and they had pulled out his fingernails, and it looked like they had stuck needles under the nails before pulling them out. When I saw his body I couldn't help but think that maybe I was next. I wouldn't be surprised if he mentioned my name as one of his friends. I don't blame him. With the horrible ways the military tortures, no one can be held responsible for what he says or does!"

We were walking toward the outskirts of town, which was quiet on this Friday night. As soon as we cleared the small houses of the alley on the outskirts of town Victor turned to me and asked, "Do you remember Alex and Juan?"

"Of course! I can't believe they're dead. You must feel terrible. They were your closest friends, weren't they?"

"Yes, but I still have one left. The one I'm talking to. You, Rica.

" I've been thinking. I could return to colegio, but I think the army has my name. They not only killed my teachers, classmates, teammates, and friends, but they also tortured some of them. I know my parents have worked hard to pay for my tuition, but I am afraid that I am next on the death squads' list. Ricardo, what should I do?"

It was a good thing we were outside of town, because I almost shouted at him. *"Es mejor que la gente diga por aqui paso, que aqui murio!"* This translates, "It is not good to stay and act macho and get yourself killed!"

BREAKING HOME TIES

Victor's father was disappointed that he had quit school, but his mother understood.

During that first week of July we began hearing from other people that Victor was in danger. My brother-in-law said he had heard from a friend in the National Police that they knew where Victor was and that they had said they were going to get him. We also learned from Tony, an old friend of mine, that his father had heard that the National Guard had blacklisted Victor, and that these records were being sent from San Miguel to San Luis.

The National Police, the death squads, and the National Guard were all branches of the army, all government troops. Tony also told me that because I was Victor's closest friend in San Luis, the army thought of us like "a pair of earrings": inseparable friends. "The National Guard wants to find the two of you and kill you in front of a lot of people to make an example of you both."

For the next two weeks, Victor and I spent all our time hiding ourselves from the army as well as from civilian informants. These informants, who were known as *dedos* (fingers), worked for the army and reported on civilian activities. We feared the dedos more than the army itself because it was difficult to find out exactly who they were.

On July 19, Victor's older brother, Mario, was killed by the Salvadoran army in the capital. Santos, Mario's father, was grief-stricken. The next day Santos piled the whole family into his truck for the drive to San Salvador for the funeral. Victor and I were afraid to get into the truck in town so about a half-hour earlier we had walked down the road so we could meet them outside of town on the way to San Salvador. The drive took about six hours, and the twelve of us arrived at the chapel that afternoon to find many other friends gathered there.

A Salvadoran's Journey

In our country it is the custom for the bereaved to stay with the deceased person continuously until the body is buried. Thanks to the friends from San Salvador, the twelve of us were able to leave for a short while so we could accept an invitation to have supper at the home of another friend of Santos.

As we were returning to the chapel, soldiers stopped our truck. Victor and I were terrified. About twenty soldiers surrounded the truck and pointed rifles and machine guns at us. I also saw numerous soldiers on a bank above us, crouched behind sandbags, with machine guns aimed at us.

We were ordered to get out of the truck, take out our ID cards, and then stand spread-eagled, with our hands against the truck and our legs spread away from the truck. The soldiers then started going down the line. When it was my turn, they kicked my legs apart more and told me to hold out my ID card. I wondered if this would be the end—of me and of all of us. I knew Victor's father was an important person in our little town, even in San Miguel the third largest city in El Salvador, but this was San Salvador, the capital.

The soldiers searched all of us, even the women, roughing up some of us. After one of the soldiers called the chapel to verify that Mario's body was there, we were finally released. We returned to the chapel to sit up with the body for the rest of the night—and to just be thankful that we had not been killed also.

After the funeral the following morning, we all returned to San Luis. That night Victor and I slept in a tamarindo tree in town. We were thankful for these trees, because their leaves provided cover and their snarled branches provided nesting places to sleep on. The next morning we walked a few blocks outside of town and hid.

BREAKING HOME TIES

We avoided the streets, jumping fences and going through people's backyards. For a few nights we were able to find some safe houses to stay in. One night we stayed with a wealthy uncle of mine, and another night we stayed in a friend's house. This was a little bit dangerous because some members of his family were in the National Guard, though they were currently stationed in other cities.

During the daytime we scrounged for food. My mind floated back to my carefree days with Tio Chente and my cousins when I was younger, when I learned to hunt with a slingshot and to catch fish with my bare hands. Victor and I were able to get enough food this way, but Victor was uncomfortable living under these conditions. He was happy, though, that I was with him, that he wasn't alone.

Only a few people knew we were even in the area. We kept very quiet because we knew that if the news of our presence in San Luis were known it might get to army ears. That Friday night was especially difficult because the town was loaded with people arriving for the next day's mercado. We decided to sleep a couple miles away, near a small river, then spent the weekend in the mountains, returning Sunday night to sleep in my grandmother's cornfield.

On Monday morning Tony dropped by the house looking for us and, not finding us, left the message with my sister that he urgently needed to talk with us. Victor and I met him on a small coffee plantation a couple blocks from Victor's house.

Tony sounded worried. "You guys already know that you are on the National Guard's black list. They said they plan to erase you from the map! The sergeant said Victor will be the next to be killed."

A Salvadoran's Journey

Victor was very upset, but even still he remembered to thank Tony for bringing us the news." We appreciate what you have done for us, Tony."

I was very worried. I said, "Victor and I don't know when we're leaving, but from what you've told us I think we should flee as soon as possible." I knew we had to make some important decisions quickly. What were our options? Did we have many choices? Were we thinking rationally? These questions were racing through my mind.

6

Breaking Home Ties

The gruesome activities of the death squads compelled Victor and me to make plans to flee El Salvador. I knew that I could escape and go into the mountains and fight with the *muchachos* (literally "kids," but the word now took on the meaning of guerrilla fighters). I, also, knew that Victor, as a student and a teenager, was not prepared for this kind of life or death situation.

A thought came to me from my calving days as a child. I remember one special friend of the family used to come and talk to us about the good life and productive agriculture in Honduras. There the harvest was good because the land was very fertile and this made life enjoyable. This friend told us that one guava in Honduras weighed ten pounds! Some people believed him, but I couldn't, because in El Salvador the land needed a lot of expensive fertilizer and even with a lot of labor the land was not very productive.

Now I thought that if I could help Victor to escape to Honduras, we could work for a while there and return home after things calmed down. Another plan could be that we could go to South America and look for work. But either way, first we needed to get across the border. Then, once in Honduras, we would need to avoid their authorities, get a passport, and find a way to support ourselves. In other words, we would have to find a way to appear to be Honduran citizens, not fleeing Salvadoran refugees.

BREAKING HOME TIES

In preparation for fleeing, we had decided that we should accept an invitation from one of Victor's classmates, who lived in La Esperanza, a small city in Honduras. Señor Velasquez had been a teacher in San Luis, and he and his wife had raised their son, Bernardo, in our hometown. Bernardo and Victor became close friends. When the political situation had heated up, they returned to their home in Honduras, telling Victor that if he ever had the need, he had an open invitation to join them there.

A few days before we actually left, right after Tony gave us the warning, we had made our way into the mountains towards the Honduran border. We went to see Elias, who was a distant relative of Victor's. He was a Honduran citizen and lived in El Salvador with his Salvadoran wife. Victor knew that Elias traveled back and forth a lot over the border into Honduras to see his family. When we arrived at his house, Elias' wife told us that he was plowing a field a couple of blocks away and asked a little boy to take us there.

We quickly introduced ourselves to him, then came straight to the point. "We came to see you because we need help. Victor has been studying in San Miguel. Most of his close friends and classmates have been killed, so he quit school and returned to San Luis. We want you to help us cross the border into Honduras. There we will catch a bus to go as deep into the country as we can get. We are willing to pay as much as you ask"

Elias didn't hesitate. "If you're ready, we can leave now," he replied.

We were relieved. I said, "We're not ready now, but later this week we'll be back, ready to go."

Under cover of darkness we stole back to San Luis and slept another night in a tamarindo tree.

A Salvadoran's Journey

Just before dawn, we awoke, climbed out of the tamarindo tree, and went home. Two weeks had gone by without sleeping in our own houses due to the war situation and the fact that the army was looking for us.

Three pairs of pants, five shirts, some underwear, and my tacos went into a backpack. That was my entire luggage when I left home—when I left my country.

While I was stuffing my backpack, my sister Beatriz stood next to the bed where my clothes were piled. I whispered to her, "I'm not sure where I should tell Abuelita I'm going. Maybe I can tell her that I'm going to the capital to look for a job."

"That's a good idea. That way she'll think that you can come home in case there's an emergency," Beatriz whispered softly.

I went back into the kitchen and sat down next to my grandmother, who was drinking her morning coffee. Beatriz brought me a plate of tamales. I suddenly realized why we were eating tamales that day. It was nine days after Victor's brother Mario's death, and there is a tradition in our country that, following a mourning period of nine days, the family and friends make and eat tamales to symbolize that life goes on. After this, the family is in a less strict period of mourning.

I couldn't speak for a while. After a long silence I started discussing the pros and cons of living in our small town versus living in a bigger city, then asked my grandmother her opinion.

She wasn't fooled for a minute. She asked, "Where are you going?"

"To San Salvador," I lied.

BREAKING HOME TIES

She gave me a sad look and replied, "I'm going to miss you."

"I will miss you, too."

"We will be waiting for you," she said. "Follow my advice and you will not have any problems." She was referring to her frequent admonition not to keep company with bad friends.

"Yes, I'll follow your advice. And I will write to you." I hugged her, and bowed my head while she blessed me.

"Remember, my son, if you don't like the new place that you are going to, know that you can always come back home anytime. We will always have something to eat here."

My eyes were full of tears. "I know, Abuelita."

Then I went back into my bedroom and picked up my backpack. I moved slowly and reluctantly out the door to the street. Then I glanced to the left and saw my uncle, Mauricio, putting a saddle on his horse and waved to him. He waved back and yelled, "Good luck !" I realized I had to move quickly now.

I hurried up the street to Victor's house. As I walked in, I saw Victor talking to his mother and grandmother. They were all crying.

"Victor, are you ready?"

"Yes, I am."

Victor went to get his backpack. His mother and grandmother approached me. I could tell from their faces they were about to say something sad.

Victor's grandmother said, "Ricardo, please take care of Victor. You are older and have more experience. Each one has to look after the other as if you were brothers."

A Salvadoran's Journey

I realized from their seriousness that Victor must have told his family that we were leaving not just our little city, but the country.

Victor emerged from his room with his pack on his shoulders and gave his grandmother and mother a long hug. With tears running down his face, he broke away from their embrace and we went out into the back courtyard where one of Victor's uncles was gardening. He got up to say goodbye. He too was serious. "I will miss you. I wish you good luck."

The date was July 28, 1980. I was twenty-seven years old, and Victor was seventeen.

We knew we could not safely walk through the streets, so we walked about six blocks through a coffee plantation to where we met my best friend, Antonio, who had warned us that the army's death squads were looking for us.

Tony looked thoughtful. He said, "I wish I were in your position, but I have a wife and two children and must take care of them." He continued, "The army says our country is too small and overpopulated, that we must kill people and say that they were Communists."

Again we thanked Tony for his help. We shook hands and bade each other *"Hasta luego."* I told Tony that I would write to him soon.

After Victor and I had walked about a kilometer, I realized that we were near the cemetery. I told Victor to wait for me and went to my mother's grave to tidy it, to say some prayers, and to cry. My throat felt tight and I couldn't swallow.

I rejoined Victor and we started hiking together towards the Honduran border… and towards an unknown world.

Part Two

7

Crossing the Border Into Honduras

Victor and I hiked fast, though cautiously. As we headed to the border, we walked through streams, over low mountains, and through valleys with dense forests. We were anxious to meet up with my cousin Concepcion, as we needed to get photos so we could get fake ID in Honduras. That night we slept at a friend's house near where we were to meet up with Conce. Early the next morning, he came, bringing the photos. He and our friend said goodbye and wished us good luck.

The sun was on our right as we traveled toward the northwest—up and away from the sun. Had we walked directly to Elias' house, we would have been there in less than three hours. But we thought it would not be safe—for either him or us—to go there directly, so our diversionary path got us there at two in the afternoon, after walking for over six hours.

Elias stood in the doorway and waved us in. We discovered that his wife had worked all day cooking corn, *tamalitos*, and *atole* (a sweet, hot, thick liquid made with corn and milk). Their table was small, but it was loaded with hot and steaming food, filling the entire little house with a wonderful fragrance. On the table there were also cujada, cheese, and cream made from fresh cow's milk. Elias' wife had made this food especially for us because she knew we were arriving that day. We felt guilty because we hadn't wanted to make more work for Elias' wife; we just wanted Elias' help getting to Honduras.

I don't know about Victor, but I hadn't sat at a table like this since *Semana Santa* (Holy Week) four months before. Now I felt safe here with this family, as I knew Elias' closest neighbors were two miles away. I decided I could relax for a few minutes, enjoy the dinner, and listen to the birds singing outside.

Our fears kept interrupting, however. Vic and I didn't know what lay ahead of us, though we knew there would be no family. We knew the loneliness would be a great contrast to our happiness at this moment.

After we finished eating, we all sat outside on some large rocks under a big tree. Elias told us that the situation in Honduras was also getting worse. Not long before there had been eight soldiers stationed in the little town of Santa Lucia, where his family lived. Now there were about fifty, and they were patrolling the border, capturing every stranger they saw. This only confirmed our feeling that we needed to hurry and heightened our worries about what lay ahead.

Before we went to bed that night, we asked Elias if he knew anyone who could make fake Ids for us. We told him we were willing to pay.

Elias said, "Yes, I have a friend at the city hall who can. It's too late right now and tomorrow is Saturday, and he usually doesn't work on Saturdays. However, I'll find him tomorrow and ask him as a special favor."

The next morning we were on our way. We were to go to Santa Lucia, then to La Esperanza, deep in Honduras. We had gone to bed early the night before, sleeping in hammocks. At four in the morning, before it was light, we got up and drank coffee and ate tamales.

A Salvadoran's Journey

Elias led the way with a small metal flashlight, walking first through cornfields and then through a forest of second growth trees I judged to be about ten or twelve feet high. By that time, the sun was just beginning to rise.

We had walked about 2.5 kilometers when we came to the Torola River, which forms the border between El Salvador and Honduras. The day was clear and, though we were low in the river valley, we could see the sun just above the mountains in front of us.

Elias stopped close to the river and said, "Wait for me here. I'm going to find my friend, Tecolote. He's going to help us cross the river."

We watched as Elias approached a small house nearby, knocked on the door, talked with Tecolote, the man who came to the door, and Elias returned to where we were standing. Here was the narrowest part of the river, where it ran between rock banks on each side. We could see the river fifteen or twenty feet below us, running very strong in the confinement of the banks.

We watched Tecolote leave his house and walk down the river about a block to where the river widened and the riverbank became a low, sandy beach. At this point the river slowed somewhat, though the current was still very strong. Tecolote stripped off his clothes and waded into the river. When he was in up to his waist, he pushed off, swimming very hard against the current pulling him downstream.

At first I wondered why we ourselves didn't just swim across. But as I watched I grew increasingly anxious for this man, as it looked like he might not make it, and realized that without a lot of practice we probably wouldn't have been able to make it across, even without our heavy backpacks.

BREAKING HOME TIES

Elias sensed my concern. "This is nothing for Tecolote," he said. "I have seen him cross this river when it was almost twice as full." Elias told me he had known Tecolote for twenty years. When Elias was a teenager, still living in Honduras, Tecolote would help him cross the river to be with his love and now his wife, who lived just across the river in El Salvador, not too far from where we were standing.

I felt a little less anxious now as I realized that Elias and Tecolote had lots of practice doing this. We saw Tecolote get to the other side about half a block down the river from where he had started, then climb up the rocks and walk back up the opposite bank until he was directly across the river from us.

Elias picked up a coil of thin rope with a rock tied to one end and swung it like a lasso. We moved away from him so he had lots of room. He tried three times before the rock landed on Tecolote's side. Elias then tied a thicker rope to the thin one and Tecolote pulled until the thick rope was on his side, where he tied it securely around a large boulder while Elias fastened his end directly in front of us to a set of posts arranged like a tripod.

By now, of course, I understood how we were going to cross the river. But at the same time as I marveled at the cleverness of this rope idea I thought about the danger. Should we fall off the rope into the river there would be no hope of survival. I looked again at the river, at how it made a sharp turn and then slammed hard against the far bank as it rounded the curve. I knew that anyone in that river would be smashed against the rocks to an instant death.

I was just starting to wonder if I'd have to cross the river hanging from the rope by my hands, when I saw Elias attach a kind of trapeze seat to the rope. The pulley wheels went on top of the thick rope and the ropes forming the seat hung down below. I was first. I sat in the seat, hanging on to a bar above my head and over the pulley. Tecolote started pulling. Besides the immediate danger of dropping off into the water, I felt like an easy target for anyone who might see me, either from the Salvadoran or Honduran armies. This Torola River had meant death for hundreds of my country people. When these unfortunate souls came to their end, holes were dug in the sand, and thousands of nameless Salvadorans lay in sand-covered shallow graves on the riverbank since 1978 when Salvadorans started crossing the river in the Morazan *departamento*. (A departamento is equivalent to a state or province.)

Once I was safely on the other side, Elias reeled in the pulley so he and Victor could cross. My relief when I got to the other side was immense. We each gave him 25 cents Salvadoran for our "crossing fee" and thanked him.

Elias again took the lead, elbowing his way through thick bushes, as we began climbing up a mountain. Elias told us that we didn't dare take the usual paths because people were coming towards us from the opposite direction.

At 8:30 a.m., after we had been traveling for about four hours, Elias stopped on top of a little hill by a stream and pointed to a small town in the distance, which he said was Santa Lucia. He continued, "I'm going into town. You two wait for me here. I'll try to get your papers, but I won't come back here. My brother will meet you here, even if I don't get the papers. He'll be wearing a rope, and he'll whistle."

Victor and I thanked Elias and watched him disappear into the woods.

BREAKING HOME TIES

Vic and I looked around a little. Though this was our first time in Honduras, the country didn't seem much different from El Salvador. Same plants, same landscape. Looking down at Santa Lucia, we could see a cemetery to the left of the town. This brought to mind a story we had heard at home in San Luis a couple of years before.

It seems that in Santa Lucia lived a very wealthy man, Señor del Cid,. The people of Santa Lucia believed he had a pact with the devil, and after he died, the pallbearers said the coffin was empty. Every day the del Cid family took food to the cemetery, and it was always gone in the morning. The story was that the devil had taken del Cid alive.

Even though we were on a hill, we didn't have to worry about drinking water because we had the stream right next to us, but as it approached noon we were getting pretty hungry. I figured that if the vegetation was similar to that in El Salvador I might be able to find something I recognized. I looked around and found some *guayavillas*, a dwarf sort of guava that is very acidic. That had to suffice for lunch. Though we were still hungry, we lay down next to the stream and took a nap.

At about five in the afternoon, we heard someone coming closer and whistling. We thought this probably was Elias' brother, but to be safe we hid behind some big trees and watched. A man with a rope on his right shoulder stopped where we had been and looked around, whistling a couple more times. Feeling sure now, I whistled back.

I moved from behind the tree and walked up to him. He said, "Hello. I'm Anselmo, Elias' brother." We shook hands, and he asked if we were hungry. "No," we said in unison. We were being polite. Nevertheless, Anselmo reached into the bag he was carrying and pulled out a loaf of sweet bread. "I have something for you anyway." We tore into the bread as if we were starving.

. Anselmo told us that Elias had been able to get only one birth certificate, the one for Victor. Victor's new name was Jesus—Jesse. Anselmo told us that the fee was twenty *lempiras* (then about ten U.S. dollars).

Anselmo said, "Let's start moving toward town. But we should not go too fast. We can't get there yet. We must go into town after dark and we must be very careful."

As we walked, Anselmo explained to us that soldiers were patrolling the town and that the people of Santa Lucia reported any foreigners they saw in the town to the soldiers.

At about seven, just as soon as possible after dark, we walked into the edge of town. We first came to a street with four or five houses on each side. Their doors were closed, but we could hear people talking. The three of us were absolutely silent.

Anselmo stopped abruptly, then whispered, "Follow me." He came to a tall barbed-wire fence with five-inch vertical spaces and climbed it like a ladder. We followed. Once over, we had to get our footing on a two-foot dirt ledge just on the other side, then jump down about nine feet to where Anselmo's house was under construction. We still had our backpacks on, so we didn't exactly feel like mountain goats.

Anselmo led us into the house through the back door. For a few minutes we just stood there, keeping very quiet. To the right, about five yards away, was a store, and through a crack in the door we could see Honduran soldiers drinking beer, laughing, and talking.

After a few minutes, Anselmo left us, explaining that he was going to his parents' house. About an hour later he returned, carrying a large bag of food. He took out some matches and lit a candle. We all sat on the floor and wolfed down cheese, beans, rice, and tortillas and gulped coffee from a bottle.

While we ate, Anselmo spoke to us in a soft voice about the arrangements he had made. "I just talked to the bus driver and the *cobrador*." The cobrador is in charge of collecting fees and selling tickets to people boarding the bus. He also stows everyone's luggage, which is placed on the top of the bus. "I told them your situation," Anselmo continued, "and they told me that often soldiers stop buses and search for people without identification. When they find anyone without papers they pull them off and interrogate them. This often happens at the exit to Colomoncagua because this is where many Salvadorans try to flee their country and come into Honduras." (Colomoncagua later became known as the Mesa Grande refugee camp.)

I interrupted Anselmo. "Victor will not have a problem, but I will because I don't have Honduran ID."

"I will talk to the cobrador, so if he or the bus driver tells you that for your safety you need to travel on top of the bus, just do it. Don't ask any questions."

The candle was still burning, but it was so dark we barely could tell the difference between beans and rice. But we didn't need to see Anselmo to know that he was not smiling as he said, "The cobrador will cover you with a tarp and tie you on the top of the bus with the chicken cages and egg baskets. This is a long trip, and they tie you so you won't fall off the top of the bus if you fall asleep."

Now he went on to explain the logistics of our next steps. He told us his parents, also, owned the house down the road. The bus itself was parked between the two houses, and they rented out the small house to the bus workers.

A Salvadoran's Journey

"The cobrador is going to knock on the door of my parents' house five minutes before midnight. By that time, you guys must be there. The cobrador will wait at the door for you. You are to walk single file behind him and get onto the bus. Victor, you will take the last seat in the back of the bus." He pointed to me. "I don't know where you are to sit. The cobrador is going to decide for you."

We were all silent for a moment, then Anselmo said, "Well, I think I've told you everything about the plans and I hope everything goes well. Welcome to Honduras and good luck."

I had been trying to think how to thank him, when it suddenly came to my mind that I had a pair of tacos in my backpack. I asked Anselmo if he played soccer.

"Yes, I'm a member of our town's team."

"What size shoe do you wear?"

As luck had it, we wore the same size. Handing him my soccer shoes, I told him, "I don't think I am going to need these where I'm going."

His face lit up. He thanked me, saying, "I was planning to buy a pair of tacos as soon as I could afford to."

By this time it was 9:30 at night. Our early-morning river crossing seemed like days before. We would have been very tired, except we were so anxious.

Anselmo whispered, "I'm going to check the streets." The store had been closed since eight and everyone was gone, so it was very quiet except for dogs barking everywhere.

In no more than five minutes Anselmo was back. "Everything's okay," he said. "Let's go."

We walked down the middle of the street, heading toward Anselmo's parents' home. The dogs in the street started to bark, but Anselmo took care of that by calling

BREAKING HOME TIES

them by name. Nevertheless we were anxious to quickly cover the three blocks left to go. When we arrived, Anselmo's mother, father, and sister were sitting around the table, their faces lit by a torch made of an old liquor bottle, half filled with gasoline, with a piece of cloth pulled through its metal cap. We later learned that the people of Santa Lucia had no electricity or generator, that they used propane lights in the evening until eight o'clock.

Victor and I said good evening and introduced ourselves. Anselmo's sister, who I guessed was about 35, said kindly, "Oh, they're so young!" Anselmo's father asked us how old we were. We replied that Victor was seventeen and I was twenty-seven.

Anselmo's father said, "Tell us about the situation in El Salvador. Why are you fleeing?"

Victor talked for a while about what was happening to himself and to the country as a whole.

The father said, "Remember this old saying: *'A terre que fueras haras lo que vieres'*—Wherever you go, do what they do."

I had heard my grandmother say that many times before, but I nodded because I knew it was especially good advice in our current situation.

Anselmo's father continued, "We usually go to bed at eight, but we wanted to meet you and wish you good luck and tell you that your decision is the best for the situation you are in." He pointed to two hammocks and said, "You have about two hours before the bus leaves. You should try to sleep or at least rest because the trip from here to La Esperanza is tiring and boring. Good night and good luck."

I took one hammock and Victor the other. I pulled off my shoes, put my backpack under the hammock, and lay down. I was extremely tired, but I couldn't sleep because my mind was on the journey ahead. I just lay there in the dark and thought.

The two hours passed as if they had been ten minutes. At the first knock on the door, we jumped up, put on our shoes, and grabbed our backpacks.

"Good morning," the cobrador said. "Let's go."

It looked like we were going to be the only people on the bus, but the cobrador instructed us to sit in the back. Pointing at me, he said, "If I think it's necessary for you to go to the top of the bus, I'll signal you." I sat in a back seat on one side and Victor on the other.

What happened next was a bit of a shock. The bus driver got onto the bus, started the engine, and began honking the horn like a lunatic. "This is crazy!" I thought. "It is midnight and this honking will wake up the whole town!" If I hadn't been so scared, I would have laughed. We had been so careful to be absolutely quiet, and now there were people coming from every direction, talking and laughing.

It turned out that this was the only bus service to and from this town. There were only 24 seats on the bus, and by the time we left the little bus was filled like a sardine can and I thought there could be no room for more. Some people brought live chickens and turkeys, stowing them in baskets under their seats. Other fowl were fastened in baskets to the roof of the bus by the cobrador.

The bus moved out slowly over the bumpy streets, stopping to pick up people waiting at other stops. By now there were between 45 and 50 people on the bus. People stood squashed together, squirming around trying to find more comfortable positions.

During the first couple of hours we were able to breathe fresh air because the windows were open wide. Later, as we drove higher into the mountains, where it was cold and the wind was blowing, they had to be closed. By this time, the air was smelly. People were smoking cigarettes and cigars, older men were chewing and spitting tobacco, and the chickens and turkeys had defecated. I didn't know how the rest of the people in the back of the bus could stand it. I felt like I was going to pass out.

I don't know what time it was when the soldiers stopped the bus at the Colomoncagua exit, but it was still dark so it must have been before four o'clock in the morning. I could see that there was a provincial station here, a small checkpoint staffed by soldiers. The cobrador, who had stood in the doorway of the bus for the entire trip, jumped off and walked over to the sergeant in charge. I watched anxiously as about fifteen soldiers surrounded the bus. "This is the end for me," I thought.

A couple of the soldiers stepped onto the bus by the driver and looked over our faces. Next to me an old man was sleeping with his hat on his lap. I carefully reached over, took the hat, and put it on my head. I wanted to look similar to the rest of the men on the bus, who all wore hats. Santa Lucia was a farming town and the men wore hats inside their homes as well as outside to protect them from the sun. Despite my former discomfort, I was suddenly glad that the bus was packed so tightly, because the soldiers were unable to walk down the aisles. After a while they gave up and got off.

My relief lasted only for a moment. Just then I looked out the window and saw the cobrador walking toward the bus with the sergeant. But the cobrador simply shook hands with the sergeant and then jumped onto the bus as the driver pulled away from the station. I started breathing again and told myself to relax.

A Salvadoran's Journey

At about 8:30 in the morning we arrived at La Esperanza, the bus's final stop and the closest city to where we were going. Everyone left the bus except Victor and me. We asked the cobrador if he knew the Velasquez family. He told us that they lived across the street from the bus driver. "If you stay on the bus, we'll be there in ten minutes."

When we stopped, the cobrador pointed across the street and said, "That's the house you're lookng for."

We could not thank the cobrador and the bus driver enough. The cobrador told us what had happened at the stop at Colomoncagua. "The soldiers didn't ask for identification because I told the sergeant that I knew everybody on the bus and that there were no strange faces." Again, we thanked him.

We were relieved to be there. It had been over eight hours since we had left Santa Lucia, and we had never gotten off the bus. We were tired and hungry, and we weren't sure if Victor's friend would be at home.

8

Life In Honduras

At our friend's house, we stood still for a few minutes longer. We knew that Bernardo would be glad to take us in, feed us, and give us a place to sleep, but what if he wasn't home. We didn't know who might answer the door.

Finally, I knocked on the door. When it was opened I asked, "Is Bernardo here?"

Bernardo was a classmate of Victor's in San Luis and was one of the sons of my first-grade teacher, Doña Velasquez. When the situation got ugly in El Salvador, she had sent Bernardo to La Esperanza to stay with aunts.

Fortunately, Bernardo was home and was glad to see us. Victor and I spent the day with him and after breakfast the next morning, we walked him to school. On the way, he said, "If you want, you can check for work at my sister Delfina's in San Antonio." I had known Delfina when she went to school in San Luis.

Bernardo told us that to get to Delfina's we needed to take a bus to Cehutepecque, then another that traveled towards San Pedro Sula. About 45 minutes before that bus would arrive in San Pedro Sula, we were to get off at the *caracol*, the Y in the road, and catch another bus, which would take us to San Antonio.

After getting off the bus in San Antonio, we walked the four blocks to Delfina's house. She was at home, but said her husband, Leonides, was not there and that she herself would not be able to help us find a job. She said she was sorry and wished us good luck.

That night the two of us slept in a wooden hut where Victor and I rented a room for the night. As we got deeper into Honduras, I felt safer from the Salvadoran authorities, yet I felt more and more lost as to the direction our lives were heading. But, then again, I thought we've only been in Honduras three days, and I didn't share these concerns with Victor, as I didn't want to upset him. There was certainly nothing he could do about this.

The following morning, I still had these gnawing thoughts. What were we going to do? What were we going to find? How were we going to live? I was anxious and worried as we put on our backpacks and started retracing our steps to San Pedro Sula—this time on foot.

Though I was anxious, we enjoyed the morning, delighting in the slight breeze at that hour of the day, walking slowly away from town, with no place in particular to go. We had covered about two kilometers towards the village of Casitas when I recognized a middle-aged woman cross the street in front of us. I Though I had forgotten her name, I knew her family. I knew that she had visited my sister Beatriz' store in San Luis de La Reina many times. I, also, knew that she had credit with Beatriz, which she had needed for flour and sugar. She lived in the countryside outside of San Luis and needed supplies to bake bread, which she sold on Saturdays at the mercado. I later remembered that her name was Doña Concha.

She recognized me. "Hola! What are you doing here?"

"We're looking for work," we pleaded, "even if it's just for food and shelter."

She asked why we were in Honduras and we told her the situation in El Salvador was getting bad so we had decided to flee the country.

She asked us, "Do you want to come inside and talk with my boss? Maybe you can stay here for a while."

We gladly followed her in and she introduced us to the couple who owned the farm, Doña Carmen and Don Benjamin."

Only Doña Carmen and Don Benjamin were in the house. It was about eight in the morning, and the rest of the men were out working, cleaning the cornfields.

Years before, I had heard that Don Benjamin had been training a mule, and when he was riding it, he fell off. The mule was bucking and Don Benjamin could not control the animal. When he fell, he hit the back of his head. From then on, he had fainting spells and seizures, though he never went to a doctor for a diagnosis. Doña Carmen managed the property and her husband stayed home because of his disability.

Doña Carmen asked us a few questions and said, "The two of you can relax for the rest of the day, then go to work tomorrow."

It turned out that Doña Concha was the maid, and she had to begin work right after she introduced us. She told us that her son Arcadio was also working there, and that he would be back at the house for lunch. I knew Arcadio and looked forward to seeing him again.

We spent the rest of the day in the backyard under the orange trees eating oranges. It was a physically comfortable time, and I felt immense relief. Not only did we both have jobs, but also, there were people around here who knew me. I was still wondering what would happen next.

BREAKING HOME TIES

Victor and I were assigned to share Arcadio's room, a small room in one of the corners of the house. The room had a door, but no curtains, and there was barely enough space for our three petates.

In the morning I went to work with Victor and Arcadio and three other men. Our job was to chop down pine trees, cut them into firewood, load the wood onto mules, and bring it back to the house. We did this for about a week or more and I grew very concerned about Victor. Working with the ax was taxing, heavy work that he was not used to, and his hands were covered with blisters.

Our crew's next job was to weed pastureland. Doña Carmen and her husband owned pastureland that they rented to a man who lived some distance from Casitas. The cattleman employed a worker named Ramon who lived in Doña Carmen's house. His job was to take care of the cows. He milked them, brought the milk to Doña Carmen's house, and took care of making the cuajada and the cheese. When his boss came every two weeks, Ramon had a 100-pound block of cheese ready for him to take to market.

The land on which the cattle were pastured was full of waist-high weeds that needed to be cut down. To chop the weeds, the workers used a special kind of machete that was a full meter long, called a *colima*. Victor and I had to buy our own colimas, which cost eight lempiras each, and we also had to buy rubber shoes, as the pastureland was swampy. All the other workers had these shoes as any other kind of shoe would not hold up. I was glad that I had enough lempiras to make these purchases. I was too proud to ask these people that I had just met for money. It just was not the way I was brought up.

74

A Salvadoran's Journey

One Sunday, I walked through a banana plantation. I was looking up at the tops of the banana plants as I walked along, strolling through weeds about two feet tall. I bent down to drink some water from a little stream and laid down my machete. I stood up, looking for ripe bananas. As I was about to scramble over a four-foot-diameter log I looked down and saw the weeds moving.

I had grown up near the countryside, where I wasn't afraid of anything—until this day. But what I saw here made me afraid. What was moving the weeds was the tail of a snake that was crawling under the log. Its head was about five feet up in the air, about four or five feet from my face, and moving toward me. The snake was over ten feet long and must have weighed fifty pounds.

I realized I didn't have my machete in my hand. I wished I had it or something even better, a rifle. I was sure this snake was going to kill me, but I thought, "I will grab it when it bites me and break its neck with my hands. That way we will both die together." For a few seconds I shivered with fear and then I held still for a minute without even moving my eyelashes. I sweated. Every ten or fifteen seconds the *barba amarilla's* tongue flicked in and out.

My eyes were fixed on the snake's eyes. I said to myself, "I'm ready and waiting for your attack."

We stared at each other for a full two minutes—minutes that seemed like hours. I did not take my eyes off the snake as it slowly recoiled down and back. I did not move. I did not breathe. I continued watching the snake. I wanted to see the entire length of the snake as it slithered away into the weeds.

When it was gone, I closed my eyes and took a deep breath. I took out my handkerchief. First, I wiped the sweat

BREAKING HOME TIES

dripping from my nose, then I wiped the salty perspiration that was running into my eyes.

As I walked back toward the stream to wash my face and pick up my machete, I thanked God for keeping me safe and for giving me the strength to defeat the barba amarilla with my eyes.

It was fun relating my story to everyone in Casitas. We had been living there for about a month when a friend of ours arrived. Camillo, another soccer teammate from San Luis, was closer to Victor's age than to mine. We were surprised to see him, but happy to see a familiar face.

After we had exchanged greetings, I asked, "What are you doing here without your wife?"

"She is with her brother in Choloma, close to San Pedro Sula," he answered. "I just came here because I heard that the two of you were here."

I had been to Camillo and Lana's wedding five years earlier. I hadn't known that Lana had a brother who lived in Honduras.

"Have you found a job in Choloma? Do you have something to do?" I asked him.

"No, but there's a big cement factory near my brother-in-law's. I'm planning to look for a job there."

Victor and I talked with him some more and carefully considered our options, whether we might also find a job. Vic and I decided to accompany Camillo to Choloma so we would be at the factory on Monday morning. That afternoon, a Saturday, we told Doña Carmen that we were going with our friend to the city to try to find a job for more money.

A Salvadoran's Journey

Victor and I still had some money left, a bit of a cushion to live on, and Camillo and I went that Monday morning to see if we could get jobs at the cement factory.

Victor went with us, but he stayed behind at the house with Lana and her brother, because he didn't feel up to looking for a job that he knew would be too difficult for him to do.

"Sorry, no jobs available today. Come back tomorrow. Maybe tomorrow there will be jobs if some workers don't show up."

While walking back to Lana's brother's house, I noticed that their big, sloped backyard was full of weeds as tall as I was. I asked if there was a reason why the weeds were so tall. "We don't have the time to cut them down," they said.

"Do you have a colima?" I asked. I hadn't brought my machete with me from Casitas, since we were thinking we were going to get jobs carrying cement bags on our backs. "I'd like to help pay for our lodgings by weeding your backyard, or at least get started on it today."

"That will be a big help to us," they said.

I sharpened the colima they gave me and went to one of the corners of the yard to start. With the first swing, I nearly choked, as clouds of dust rose from the leaves. I realized then that the cement factory was only two or three blocks from the house and that dust from there had blown onto everyone's property. I tied a handkerchief around my face and mouth and continued working. I must have looked like a bandit.

I slashed weeds the rest of the day, and that night Victor, Camillo, and I went fishing. But when we got to the lagoon we found that there were clouds of *zancudos* (long-legged mosquitoes). They started biting us on our backs

BREAKING HOME TIES

and sucking blood. We ran as if we had seen the devil. We weren't able to go into the water at the lagoon, so we returned to Camillo's brother-in-law's house.

For the next three mornings Camillo and I went to the factory to check for employment. Then we gave up and started talking about what we were going to do next. I knew that Doña Carmen had properties up on a mountain called La Nieve, that she had a house in the middle of a coffee plantation. Besides the coffee plantation, Doña Carmen and her husband had other land nearby that I thought could be cultivated to grow almost anything. The four of us—Camillo, Lana, Victor, and I—decided to ask Doña Carmen and Don Benjamin if they would let us stay up there so we could work for ourselves.

We three varones left Choloma and returned to Casitas to talk with Doña Carmen and Don Benjamin. They were happy to hear that we wanted to do this and said we would be doing them a favor by taking care of the house as it was only used during the coffee-picking season, which lasted only a month and a half out of each year.

Camillo returned immediately to Choloma to get Lana, and Victor and I started preparing for the move. We bought beans (some for planting, some for eating), dried corn (mostly for eating), coffee, sugar, rice, salt, cheese, sardines in a tin, cigarettes and matches, and plenty of sharpening files for our machetes. Most of these things we paid for with cash, but the sardines, cheese, and beans we were able to obtain on credit from Delfina. I think she felt good about giving me the credit because my sister in San Luis had always given credit to her mother.

We were out of money and in debt, but we had what we needed to live on for the next 15 days. We would survive in our new environment.

A Salvadoran's Journey

Maybe we could find wild fruits and berries. Maybe there would be streams around that had freshwater crab and fish in them, or maybe there were wild animals that we could hunt with our slingshots.

Though I had only heard of this place and had never been there, to me this would be an adventure. I knew that the closest neighbor to this house on La Nieve was about two miles away, so I felt like I was going into the wilderness. I knew I was going to have to work hard, but that I would have a good time up on the mountain.

9

Another Goodbye

When it was cloudy and rainy on the mountain, Victor and I would get pensive and nostalgic for home. We continued talking about traveling south, maybe to Costa Rica or South America, hoping that we could find a place for a better future. Ever since we had left San Luis, this had been our hope and dream, a place to live until we could return to our own country. We both missed a more civilized life with people around us, with easier access to medicine, a social life, and sports. Our main concern on this mountain was to clear some land and plant red beans. Then, when we weren't working for ourselves, we weeded and cleaned the coffee plantation. We only got paid for the weeding job. We worked very hard and saved every penny, trying to cheer each other up by planning the journey south.

Every week I wrote home to my sister Beatriz. I didn't use my own name on the envelope, but I did sign "Ricardo" inside. All of San Luis must have known where we were and what we were doing, so we were not completely surprised when Gregorio knocked on our door.

Gregorio was a man in his mid-thirties who had family living in the Pacific Northwest. He was born in Honduras to Don Benjamins' brother and a Salvadoran mother. He grew up living in both San Luis and Honduras. He had come to the mountain on his way north. It wasn't difficult to get a visa from Honduras to Mexico, and from there

BREAKING HOME TIES

Greg hoped to travel to the U.S. to work, make some money, and then return to El Salvador to live comfortably.

Gregorio thought he would be able to earn enough money to do this by weeding the coffee plantation for a week. We told him that we were paid 35 lempiras a field. A field—or *manzana*—is 50 *brazadas* square. A brazada is the length of a man's outstretched arms from fingertip to fingertip, so about a hundred meters square. It's difficult to compare this broken land on a mountainside to a flat piece of land.

Gregorio was in very good shape and thought that weeding was simple, consisting of bending over and using a large machete to cut the weeds at ground level. He looked over our fields and bragged, "I can do a manzana a day. This is going to be easy money!" Victor and I glanced at each other. It had taken us a whole week to do one manzana.

After three days, having worked from 6 a.m. to 6 p.m., Greg came to our room saying he was very tired and that he had only finished half a manzana. Again Victor and I glanced at each other. We didn't laugh aloud because we knew that Gregorio had a bad temper and we figured he would have started a fight.

The next day Victor and I rose at the usual time, made coffee, and had our breakfast of fried beans. Usually Greg was the first to get up, but not this morning. I went to his bed and woke him. But when he tried to get up he couldn't. In fact, he couldn't even sit up. He said, "I've got a terrible pain in my back and I need to go outside."

I called Victor and the two of us helped Gregorio to the bushes. Vic and I couldn't help laughing to ourselves. Here we were, after only three days, helping the "macho man" relieve himself in the bushes. We took him back to bed and brought him coffee and some bananas from the kitchen, where we always had ripe bananas hanging.

Victor and I were working close to the house so we returned at lunchtime. Greg was still in bed, moaning. Victor remembered the old idea of heating glasses and placing them on Gregorio's back. It reminded me of a scene in the movie *Zorba the Greek,* though to me it was much funnier. After the hot-glass treatment Vic massaged Greg's back.

A few days later Greg was again walking by himself. One afternoon after Victor and I finished working Gregorio told us more about his plans to go the United States and asked Victor if he would like to travel with him, saying that he was afraid to travel alone and wanted company. Victor said, "Let me think about it."

That night Victor and I talked about Gregorio's idea. Victor said, "Rica, in the first place, I don't have enough money." He hesitated, then asked, "Would you mind if I went with Greg and left you here?" Victor said he was feeling reluctant to leave because we had left home together and had made all our plans together.

"I don't mind. I can manage on my own," I answered, "but are you prepared to travel with someone you don't know very well?" I was worried about Gregorio's temper and Victor's stubbornness.

Victor thought for a moment. "I'm not sure, but I know that I'm getting tired of this place. Gregorio told me that he has enough money to get me as far as Mexico, but that first I would have to travel from here to the capital, Tegucigalpa, to get a passport and a visa to Mexico. If I spend 50 lempiras for the passport and 10 lempiras for the visa plus whatever I have to pay for the round-trip bus fare, I will be penniless."

BREAKING HOME TIES

"Well, for our work together our patron, Doña Carmen, owes us 185 lempiras, which we are supposed to divide fifty-fifty. I don't mind if I'm penniless here, because I get three meals a day and a floor to sleep on. Let's ask for our money and you can have it all for your trip."

I stopped for a breath, then asked, "But do you really want to go to the U.S.?"

"No, I just want to go to Mexico."

I didn't entirely believe him. Although I didn't want to be left alone with strange people, I didn't want to stand in his way. Victor wasn't used to working like this, not used to eating tortillas and beans and sleeping on a flea-infested mat on a concrete floor for three months. I didn't have any money, and, mainly, I had no desire to go north. Besides, I had not been invited to go along.

A couple of days later we said goodbye and good luck and, as they walked out of sight, I yelled, "Write me!" I was worried because Victor was so young, and I had been entrusted by his family to look out for him.

About a month after Victor and Gregorio left I was felling pine trees and cutting them up into firewood for processing sugarcane. I was doing this near Doña Carmen's cane plantation. This firewood was later collected and taken to the *trapiche*, a hut where the cane is processed. Once we had enough firewood ready, we would gather the sugarcane. Fires would be built under big vats of juice extracted from the sugarcane, which needed to boil for hours and hours to start to thicken. I knew there had to be plenty of firewood, since the process couldn't be stopped in the middle while we gathered more. One can't stop this process until the syrup is ready to be put into the mold.

A Salvadoran's Journey

I heard shouts from up on the hill. I looked up and saw, my nephew Natan and my primo, Conce I was so happy to see both young men, yet afraid they might have bad news from El Salvador. I realized that they knew how to find me because of the letters I had written to my sister Beatriz.

I had worked up a sweat, so I had taken off my shirt and was standing there with my axe in my hand. Natan said that I looked really good—muscular and well fed. I laughed and asked them, "What winds have blown you here, guys? Is everything okay at home?"

"We heard from your letters that this is paradise, so we came to see for ourselves," Conce said.

I asked about everyone, especially my grandmother. They told me everybody in the family and all our friends were fine except for Manuel, a teacher and, also, a soccer teammate of mine, who had been killed in his apartment. My 22-year-old cousin Eladio, who had been lying in a hammock talking with Manuel, had also been shot (inches above the heart). He had gone limp, faking being dead. After the three killers left the apartment Eladio ran towards his parents' house. He made it only half a block before he fainted in the street. My aunt and uncle found him and took him to the hospital. Eladio survived.

Manuel, the teacher, had been born in San Salvador, and his family still lived there. They came to pick up the body and take it back to bury it near their home, and before they left San Luis they tried to find out what happened. They learned that the shooting had happened in broad daylight at about noon, right in front of children and townspeople. It was common knowledge that the killers were 3 National Guardsmen dressed in civilian clothes that lived in the front part of Manuel's apartment house. Manuel's parents asked everyone, "Did anybody see

BREAKING HOME TIES

anything or hear the shots?" and they all answered, "We didn't see or hear anything." Later they went to see Eladio in the hospital and asked him, too, if he knew who had shot their son. Eladio said, "I don't know who they were." I think Eladio lied—because he was afraid the men would return to kill him, his parents, and the rest of his family.

Manuel's family could do nothing. They must have suspected the National Guard, but without witnesses they could only take their son home and sadly bury him. Hearing this story. My mind jumped back to the circumstances surrounding Calendria's murder and his grief stricken mother.

Apparently, the situation in El Salvador had deteriorated even more since I had left in the summer, as Conce and Natan told me about many more incidents like the one involving Manuel and Eladio. This depressed me because I had been thinking of going back when the situation improved and now it sounded as if it was getting worse.

Conce and Natan had both graduated from high school in San Miguel in the fall, so I was not surprised when they said they had obtained Honduran birth certificates in order to get their passports so they could continue on their way north.

I finished chopping wood a few days later. The cane was processed, and now it was time to pick coffee. About thirty workers came to the mountain, La Nieve, to pick coffee, and joined Conce, Natan, and me. Natan and Conce stayed and picked for a week or so, then went down into town to visit people they knew while I stayed on the mountain and continued working. The two of them never took the twelve-hour trip back up the mountain again.

A Salvadoran's Journey

My main job was to de-shell the picked coffee beans. Doña Carmen had raised five children, four sons and a daughter. Daniel, her only biological son, was thirty years old and an alcoholic. The previous harvest, Daniel had been in charge of taking the coffee down the mountain to his mother's house to be sold. She found out that he was unloading half the sacks at the house and then taking the rest into town and selling them for half price to buy liquor. This year Doña Carmen gave Daniel's job to one of her adopted sons, Domingo, and I had taken Domingo's job as de-sheller.

The pickers would bring hemp sacks to the yard next to the house where I was working. Each sack weighed between 150 and 200 pounds depending on how easy it was to gather the beans. Doña Carmen checked to see that the workers included only ripe red beans. Green beans were worthless and should not have been mixed in with the red ones. The pickers tried not to mix in some green ones to fill their buckets faster, because they would have to remove them anyway. The workers emptied their sacks into buckets and Doña Carmen kept track of how many buckets each man had picked. Each five-gallon bucket held about 25 pounds, and the going rate was 30 cents per bucket, so three buckets totaled about one lempira. In El Salvador the coffee plants were pruned into bushes, but here in Honduras the coffee trees hadn't been pruned, so the trunks were a foot across and 10 to 12 feet high, so it could be quite difficult to pick fast. But if the picker was fast and the trees were full, he could earn two lempiras a day, which was very good pay.

After Doña Carmen's inspection, the pickers would dump the full buckets onto a tarp in a mound. I would scoop up a bucket from this volcano of red coffee beans

BREAKING HOME TIES

and place it in a big bin on the pulp grinder. This grinder had a big handle on one side, which I turned by hand. While I cranked, water would run into the bin through a hose from above. The de-shelled coffee beans would go out the front and the separated pulp would go out a gutter on the side. In El Salvador this was all mechanized. In Honduras it was all 'Ricardo-arm-power.'

I was paid by the day—from 6 to 6—earning two lempiras a day, which was good pay since few pickers made more than one and a half lempiras a day. Also, the pickers couldn't work when it rained, but I could. It rained on and off year-round at that elevation and this time of year had even more rain. I just wore my shorts and cranked away.

In the evening I would be proud to see a tall volcano of de-pulped coffee, though not as tall as the one I had started with. I would cover the pile with a tarp, and the next morning when I saw the sun coming up—about six o'clock—I would carry the beans in a wheelbarrow to a concrete slab and spread them out to dry. The slab had a 3-inch lip around it, so the coffee wouldn't roll out. Several slabs of coffee were already drying there as it takes about three days to dry. When dry, we packed the beans into 100-pound sacks and loaded them in pairs on horses or mules to carry down the mountain to Doña Carmen's house, where she marketed the coffee.

While I was living on Mt. Nieve, an old lady named Fernanda (we called her "Nanda") lived there, too. She was a coffee picker, about 60 or 65 years old, who didn't have a home. Sometimes she lived with her daughter, but when they had conflicts Nanda moved to Doña Carmen's house on the mountain, where Nanda knew she was always welcome. Besides eating there, Nanda had a few shots of liquor when Doña Carmen herself was imbibing. Doña Carmen stayed on the mountain with us during harvest time. All thirty people slept at this house, with a dozen or so sleeping outside. Don Benjamin was the only one left at home. Everybody else was up on the mountain.

After we became friends I would tease Nanda. On the weekends, while everyone was sitting around in the living room, I would walk in and ask Nanda for permission to go to town. I would say, "Don't worry, my love, I will be back soon." I would say this in a serious voice and I wouldn't smile. Everyone would laugh.

Sometimes Nanda would say, "What the hell are going to do in town? Everything that you could need or want is right here."

I'd always invent some excuse to convince her. The rest of the people would laugh and I'd walk out, still very serious-looking.

When Nanda was picking coffee, I'd take a break from my job and carry in the coffee she had picked. When we'd finish working in the evening, she'd say, "Thank God there were other people around this afternoon or you might have mistaken me for the bag of coffee you had on your shoulders."

"I just wanted to see if you would resist or if you were ready to take a ride to the woods."

"I told you—after we kiss in front of the priest."

"Okay, okay. Let's save every penny to make this thing big."

She'd fire back, "That's why I'm on these hills like a mountain goat picking coffee!"

We made everyone laugh. Even though we didn't have a TV or even a radio, all of us were entertained.

BREAKING HOME TIES

When we first came up on the mountain to pick coffee, Doña Carmen sent a pig with us, to be slaughtered for a feast when we finished picking. During the three weeks we lived on the mountain, the pig ate the workers' excrement. The pig didn't have much success. It was still as skinny as a dog.

A few days before Christmas, after I had been de-shelling for about two weeks, the workers finished picking the coffee and the next morning at ten I finished, too. Earlier that morning, while I was still grinding, watching my volcano disappear, I had heard pig squeals. I brought the last batch to the slab, emptied it on top of the other beans, and let out a loud screech—eeeeiiiiiiii. The sound traveled across the valley and bounced off the other mountains and continued echoing. Everyone ran to see what the hell had happened. "I finished!" I yelled. I started laughing and everyone joined in.

I washed up, put away my tools, and joined the crowd of workers for a cup of coffee. I had a chance now to see what everyone else was doing. One man took down the last part of the pig, which had been hanging by its hind legs in a tree. The women were in the house starting the barbecue. They had skewered the strips of pork with an *espeton*, a wavy metal skewer. These espetons were placed over coals in a horseshoe-shaped open barbecue pit, a *hornilla*. We spent all the rest of the day and most of the evening eating barbecued pork and tortillas, drinking coffee, and talking. For a skinny pig, it tasted good.

The next morning after breakfast we packed up everything, including all the kitchen utensils. We soaked the beans that hadn't dried yet to keep them from rotting and loaded these and the kitchen equipment on all the horses we had. The other workers returned to their own

90

homes, and Camillo and his wife Lana and I went down to Doña Carmen's house where we were invited to stay until we could find another place. We met Conce and Natan who had been to the capital getting passports and visas to Mexico and visiting classmates whose parents lived in Honduras. They derived some modest pleasure in seeing friends who had also fled the war in El Salvador.

A couple of days before Christmas, we were sitting on the patio in front of the house when a bus stopped right in front of us. We were delighted to see Natan's thirteen-year-old brother, Herbert, and Conce's great aunt get off the bus. We jumped up to help carry their luggage—six large bags! It reminded me of when I used to travel with my grandmother. She would take so many bags it seemed as if the only things she didn't take were the bed frames. We lugged the stuff into the room where we slept with some other workers, everyone talking at once. We were so happy to see family from our hometown!

Herbert opened one of the bags and said to me, "We brought things for you, Tio, and for Natan and Conce." For all of us they sent some dried beef and a couple pounds of cheese. My special presents were a pair of light-green Hush Puppies and a pair of blue jeans. These gifts were especially welcome because, since I had arrived in Honduras I had bought only the things I absolutely needed—a pair of rubber boots, a hat, and a machete. These are the things I needed, and two lempiras a day was not a lot of money.

We bombarded our new visitors with questions about the family and were relieved to hear that everyone was fine. We took Herbert to a little store about two blocks away to buy pop. This store, called a *trucha*, was an after-work

BREAKING HOME TIES

gathering place for the men, where they played cards, talked, and told the stories of the day. This was the first time Herbert had been included with the men. We stayed for a short time and then returned to Doña Carmen's just before dark, in time to go to sleep.

The next day was Christmas Eve. That afternoon Conce, Natan, Herbert, and I went to visit our friends Leonidas and Delfina in San Antonio, about three miles from the ranch. Delfina was the owner of the store and had given me credit when I first went up the mountain and came to Doña Carmen's which I paid off by selling her the red beans Victor and I had planted. We were surprised to find Delfina's mother, Doña Velasquez, visiting, the one who been the first-grade teacher in San Luis. She had brought her two younger sons with her as well as Natan's teenage cousin Henrique who we learned would have been in grave danger had he stayed in El Salvador.

We were a big group and we all started laughing and talking at once. All seven of us guys went for a walk through the town and stayed for a while in a park in the center of town then returned to Delfina's house and ate tamales.

Afterwards we went to visit Leonidas' brother and parents who lived a block away from the store. We enjoyed our visit, and the time went by quickly. At about seven o'clock we heard music coming from the center of the town, a few blocks away. We seven guys decided to see what was going on at the *casa communal*, where the town dances were held. On our way, we stopped at a store and everyone chipped in to buy a fifth of J&B whisky. We continued walking until we reached a dark alley. We opened the bottle and had a shot (really a gulp) each. There were just seven shots in the bottle and I was the last.

A Salvadoran's Journey

By the time we got to the casa communal, there were already a lot of people inside. Natan, Henrique, and one of Doña Velasquez's sons decided to go in, but the rest of us decided not to because the admission fee was 8 lempiras! I had enough money, but I was not interested in dancing. The reason it was so expensive was that the group was from San Pedro Sula and this was the first time they had played in this town. Also, it was Christmas Eve. There was no cost for listening outside, so the other four of us stayed outside listening to the music until 3:30 in the morning.

On our way back to Doña Carmen's house, we had walked less than a mile when we saw three men blocking the road and holding meter-long machetes. We kept walking toward them, trying to be as casual as possible. I heard one of them say, "This is the end of you guys."

I yelled to the others, "Grab some rocks!"

Gracias a Dios, there were more rocks than anything else here. While I was yelling I sent a rock flying to the man in the middle. I didn't hit him, but the rock passed close to his face. When he felt the wind, he turned and started running away, with the other two following close behind. I ran after them, picking up rocks and throwing them as I ran. They ran like they had seen the devil.

I continued running and throwing rocks. My family was running beside me, but they started laughing as they saw the men running away. "Stop laughing and throw more rocks," I scolded them.

We ran two more blocks, then slowed down, keeping a rock in each hand just in case. All the way to Doña Carmen's we walked in the center of the road.

While I calmed down, I had time to reflect on the fact that this was the first time I had not been in San Luis going to church on Christmas Eve.

10

Mountain Of Dreams

It had been a wonderful Christmas, despite being away from home, but at this point in my life I was uncertain what to do next. But I was strong and knew that I could continue to work to make a new life. I didn't know yet what form my dreams would take, but I had high hopes. With the work for the season caught up, I decided to move on.

From Doña Carmen's in Casitas I headed south to La Esperanza. I stayed a couple days in La Esperanza and spent some time looking for work. But it was a cold, windy place, and my clothes were not appropriate for that climate in January. I was almost glad that I didn't find any work.

I had heard that another friend from San Luis, Manuel Vasquez, one of Conce's relatives, was living in the mountains of Colon, a Honduran state that borders on the Atlantic Ocean, in a little town called Aldea Rio Chiquito.

The bus route first went north and east to Siguatepeque, then to San Pedro Sula. In the terminal I changed buses to Tela, situated right on the Atlantic Ocean. From La Esperanza it was going to take nine hours. During the ride from San Pedro Sula, I befriended an older man who was on his way to Tela, trying to find his sister whom he hadn't seen since childhood. He must have been as weary as I because he had started out from Marcala, a little town south of La Esperanza. He asked if I had any family in Tela, and I said, "No, I'm going farther." I asked him where he was sleeping that night, thinking that maybe we could share a room.

"I have an old friend in Tela," he said. "Maybe he can give us shelter for the night."

La Ceiba is a medium-sized city. The land is flat, and I saw a lot of pineapple plantations. We got off the bus and walked around Tela trying to find the old man's friend. His friend was a writer of books and poetry and was very popular all over town, so we found him easily. Luckily he agreed to let us stay at his house overnight. I slept in a hammock at his house, and ate with his family.

The next morning I got up early, but waited until my hosts arose so I could thank them and say goodbye to them and to the friend I had made on the bus. Then I took two buses to Bonito Oriental, about 5 hours from La Ceiba, where I began asking how to find my friend, Manuel. I found someone who knew that Manuel came to get his mail at this town's small dry goods and supply store, so I went in and introduced myself to the owner.

"I'm a friend of Manuel Vasquez from El Salvador. Can you tell me how to get to his house in Aldea Rio Chiquito?"

"Manuel lives up on the mountain," he said. "I could take you, but it's about an eight- or ten-hour walk so we'd have to wait until tomorrow, and since it'll be Sunday, somebody from up there will probably be down to buy supplies for the month, so maybe you could walk up the mountain with whomever comes down."

"That sounds like a good plan," I said. "But is there some place for me to spend the night? Something like a hotel or pension?"

He smiled. "There's no such thing in this small town. If you don't mind, you can spend the night out back in my granary."

I grinned and told him that this wouldn't be the first time I had slept on corncobs.

He led me to a small storehouse about the size of a 10-by 12-foot room. The building was supported with concrete blocks a couple feet off the ground to keep small rodents from eating the corn and to keep the granary dry when the rains came. Also, about a dozen pigs were living underneath the structure.

I left my backpack inside and went back to the store to buy a bag of bread and a bottle of pop. This had to do for dinner.

There wasn't much else to do except wait. I walked across the street and explored a flat dirt field used as a landing strip for light airplanes, then walked back to the granary and sat in the doorway. I was feeling sad and sort of sorry for myself, wishing I could go back home to San Luis.

As soon as it got dark a swarm of zancudos started biting me. I jumped up and closed the door before any more could come in. In Central America there are two kinds of mosquitoes. The one we call mosquito is small and bites during the daylight. Zancudos are bigger and bite at night. They have long legs and a visible stinger that can get through three layers of clothing to suck a person's blood. I was tired from traveling and fell asleep despite the zancudos flying next to my ears.

I awoke early. I bought some more bread for breakfast, and the storeowner's wife offered me a cup of coffee. By seven o'clock I was ready, with my backpack in hand, waiting impatiently to see if Manuel or anyone else would come.

After a while, the storeowner told me that I should relax because it would be at least noon before anyone would arrive from Aldea Rio Chiquito.

He guessed correctly. Just after noon, a man walked into the store and the owner called me over and introduced us. I learned that his name was Juan Barahona. I asked him if he knew Manuel Vasquez.

"Yes, I know him. He lives just a few blocks from my house."

"Do you mind if I go with you to Manuel's house?"

"No problem. I'd be glad to have the company."

Juan had a list of supplies he needed written on a scrap of paper. It didn't take him more than ten minutes to gather his goods together and put them into a burlap sack.

He turned to me. "Are you ready? Let's go."

I thanked the storeowner and his wife and Juan and I walked out of the store. Juan threw his sack over his shoulder and I followed with my backpack on my back.

The first part of the journey was over a flat plain with scrub bushes, and trees no taller than ten feet high. We walked for about half an hour through calf-high puddles of mud. My shoes were only ankle high, so the water and mud ran down my legs into my shoes, but I tried not to pay attention to my discomfort. I just made sure my shoes were tied tightly so I wouldn't lose them, and walked as fast as I could. Sometimes when I could catch up with him, Juan talked to me.

"I usually don't come to town, but I had to come to get medicine," he explained. "My wife has been sick with a fever for three days and my young son has had diarrhea for a week."

A Salvadoran's Journey

About four in the afternoon, I was about half a block behind and Juan stopped to wait for me. He said he was getting hungry. He looked around and spotted some wild sugarcane plants. He cut a cane from the trunk of one and then cut it into two pieces. The top meter or so he stuck into the ground to grow again, as is the custom. The other two meters were to eat. We each cut two stalks. We didn't stop. We walked while eating sections of cane.

We crossed many streams, encountering more as we went higher. Sometimes the road crossed over the streams, and sometimes just followed along. I was glad I had a guide, because I would never have found my way because the road went up and down the streams.

I've been calling it a road, but it was more like a trail as it was only for people and horses, not cars. Juan said, "We are lucky. It hasn't rained for two days, so the rivers and streams are low." He explained that sometimes pack horses got stuck in the mud because of their weight. The only way to get them out was to remove their packs and pull them out. It usually took a couple of men to do this.

By five o'clock I was dizzy, sweating, and tired. I asked, "Are we at least half way there?"

"Oh, yes. We're close now," he said.

A little later we crossed a small river then walked the equivalent of two blocks and crossed another river. I later noticed that these two rivers met at a Y to form one big river, but it was easier to cross the two smaller rivers.

Suddenly Juan said, "We are here in Aldea Rio Chiquito."

I looked around and saw only two houses—one to my left and one to my right. I was relieved to be there, but it turned out that we still had a kilometer to walk.

BREAKING HOME TIES

Finally we came to a Y in the road and Juan stopped and pointed to the right. He said, "That's Manuel's house over there. My house is to the left."

I shook his hand. "Thank you for being patient with my slowness. I hope the medicine makes your wife and child feel better."

We separated and I walked up a little hill, crossed a stream, and, just at dusk, knocked on Manuel's door.

"Who is it?" I heard Manuel say.

I told him my name.

Manuel yanked open the door. He was surprised and pleased to see me, but pulled me immediately into the house, quickly closing the door behind us.

"Is there some bad news from my family? Or are you hiding from the law?"

I laughed and assured him that there was no bad news.

It was good to be back with a family again. Manuel's wife brought us some food and drinks while Manuel told me that they had moved to the mountain with their six children about eight months before. He said that they had moved from Casitas, where Doña Carmen and her family lived.

I filled him in on the events in my life over the past six months.

"I felt alone in Casitas," I told him. "My relatives and other friends who were staying at Doña Carmen's left heading north. I'm not interested in going north. I'd like to earn some money here and continue south if the situation in El Salvador stays bad. You're one of the only people I know here in Honduras. Can I stay with you for a while? I'll work and help you in exchange for room and board."

"Yes, that's okay. You can stay as long as you want because I can use the help. Since I've moved here, I've become an *aserrador*. I lost my partner a month and a half ago. Would you like to try being my new partner?"

An aserrad*or,* I knew, is half of a two-man logging team. He fells trees, then cuts them into the desired lengths, planes the wood, and even takes the logs to market. An aserrador is more like a lumberjack than a logger because there is no sawmill or mechanization involved. I had watched this cutting process on Salvadoran-sized trees but never on the huge trees that grow in Honduras. I knew I would learn a lot, which would take my mind off some of the loneliness I felt.

"I'd be happy to give it a try," I said eagerly.

The following morning we met up with another team of two men. Manuel introduced me to Cristobal and Arturo. The four of us hiked through a valley, across a river and a few streams, over the foothills, and up a big mountain (or *sierra*). This Honduran, Cristobal, reminded me of the name of my boyhood friend in San Luis who had worked for Santiago.

As we walked I grew more anxious. Around Manuel's house none of the trees were much higher than a single-story house, about 15 feet high. Now, in front of us, lay a pristine virgin mountain with 75-foot-tall trees. Only scattered rays of sunlight penetrated through the canopy, and the forest floor was covered about a foot deep in wet leaves. I saw fresh footprints of armadillos, *tepeizcuinte*, deer, *dantes* (tapirs), and boars. Up in the trees were different kinds of tropical birds, monkeys, and *pezotes* (a member of the badger family). I felt I was in heaven with all the different sounds—the birds and the animals and the rushing water. It seems contradictory, but somehow there was the sound of stillness, as in dense forests everywhere.

BREAKING HOME TIES

Speaking quietly, Cristobal told us about how he had killed a mountain lion in this forest. He had been living in the deepest part of the mountain forest, hunting with a rifle and eight dogs. One morning on his way to work, he heard his dogs barking and chasing something across the cornfield. This wasn't unusual as almost every morning they had picked up the scent of some animal that had been in the fields overnight. Most often they ended up chasing armadillos or a tepeizcuinte. This paca looks like a short-eared rabbit, but is really a member of the rodent family weighing about thirty pounds.

On other days, when Cristobal got to the dogs they were pawing the ground, digging, and barking. But this particular morning Cristobal had a big surprise. The dogs were looking up a tree and on the lowest branch was a mountain lion looking down at him.

Cristobal shot the lion and it fell from the tree, though it was still alive. The first two dogs that went for it got badly scratched. Cristobal shot the animal twice in the head, then dragged the carcass to a nearby stream, where he skinned it. Cristobal said he had just sold the pelt for the equivalent of twelve and a half dollars.

Now the the four of us spent the next two hours selecting trees, one for each team. Manuel showed me what to look for. To get the best price at the marketplace the tree needed to be a very big, tall, straight mahogany, with no hidden cracks or hollow spots. This selection was a difficult task, as there were countless varieties of trees, many of which were oaks, though it was interesting that there were no pine trees as in Casitas or La Esperanza. These criteria were strict, and as an added burden this perfect tree had to be close to the river so we could float the lumber to market.

A Salvadoran's Journey

Manuel and I were lucky to find a tree that was lying on the ground with half its roots in the air and half still in the ground. We walked around the tree checking for knotholes or cracks. It was a good tree.

The base of the tree was about 7 feet in diameter. We would use the first 25 feet and leave the last 12 or so feet, as they had branches on them and were not suitable for lumber.

We returned to Manuel's house and spent most of the afternoon sharpening our tools. Manuel had two axes and one 8-foot, two-man saw, called a *barrilete*. Each tooth of the barrilete had to be hand filed one tooth at a time, following the direction of the alternating teeth.

The next day we arose at 5 am, had a big breakfast, and headed for the forest. Because our tree was already on the ground, I watched for a moment while Cristobal and Arturo began felling their tree. They each used an ax that was about a meter long, with a head that weighed five pounds. Their tree also was about seven feet across so that their ax handles were just big enough to span half of the tree's diameter. One swung first overhand, then underhand. Working steadily it took them the whole day to fell their tree.

Meanwhile, we used the barrilete to trim off the ragged bottom, so we could start with a straight surface.

The tree was lying across the mountain but would not roll downhill because the branches were still on it. Using some of the larger branches, we built a provisional ramp on the downhill side of the trunk. I stood on that and Manuel cut from the upper side. It took us all day to make the cut straightening up the base of the tree that we had to cut from the roots.

BREAKING HOME TIES

We had to build a platform just underneath the downhill side of the trunk that would eventually hold the first 12-foot section we would cut. Manuel explained that if we just cut off part of the tree and did not provide a platform, the section would just roll down the hill into the river. .

To build this platform, we first cut four posts from part of the tree's branches and "planted" these in pairs at the sides of the 8-foot sections. We dug the four holes with a *barra*, a steel rod four feet long and two inches in diameter that resembles a crowbar. One end of the barra is pointed like a pencil and the other end is flat and trapezoidal like the head of a screwdriver or a flat shovel. Next we cut up some of our tree's longer branches, ending up with logs about ten inches in diameter to use as a ramp. These we laid to fit across the rectangle made by the posts, with the long dimension running horizontally across the hillside.

We next measured off 12 feet of the tree and marked where we would cut. So we could guide the section we were going to cut off onto the platform, we fashioned a simple kind of pulley around the 12-foot section. To do this, we tied about 80 feet of four-inch rope around a large stick. We dug under the tree with the stick, and as we dug we pushed it and the rope under the tree. Uphill about 30 feet from our log were two smaller trees. We cut off another branch from our tree, about 7 feet long and 15 inches in diameter, and placed it horizontally spanning the uphill side of the two trees. We then wrapped the rope around the branch, securing it by tying the end around still another branch, which we drove into the ground uphill from the horizontal branch.

A Salvadoran's Journey

A Logging Platform

BREAKING HOME TIES

The last step before cutting off the first 12-foot section was to place two logs at the base of our mahogany tree, slanting downward to rest on the platform at about a 45-degree angle. This would serve as a ramp for the section to travel on after it was cut. You can imagine from these careful preparations how heavy that 12-foot by 7-foot section of log must have been.

It rained all day as we worked. We drank water from a dried gourd that we had brought with us, sucked on sugarcane from a nearby field, and ate the food that Manuel's wife had packed for us

Finally we could begin sawing! The two of us started sawing the section at six in the morning, and at two o'clock in the afternoon, when we had only about eighteen inches more to cut, we called the other team over to help. After we finished the cut, we had to move fast. Cristobal and Arturo each held one side of the horizontal limb forming the pulley, while Manuel and I positioned ourselves downhill from the tree. Manuel was about five feet further down than I was. I was directing and guiding the log on my side, and Manuel was doing the same on his. The other team slowly let the rope unwind and Manuel and I watched until the log was resting on the slanted skids. When Cristobal and Arturo felt the rope lose tension, they knew that the log was resting nearly in place. We knew that it was dangerous. We were sweating because we were working so intensely, but we knew we had to brace the log to keep it from rolling. From the uphill side the four of us used long poles as levers to push the tree onto the platform, then secured it in place with four wedges on each side, two on the downhill side and two on the uphill side. Manuel and I were ready to jump out of the way if anything should go wrong.

A Salvadoran's Journey

From there Manuel and I could handle it by ourselves, so the other guys went back to their own log. Again we had to do more preparation before we could continue. First we dug a ditch under the platform so that one of us could stand in the ditch and saw from below while the other person sawed from above. To be sure we could make a very straight cut through the tree we needed to mark a line all the way around the tree. Manuel used a hinged wooden measuring tape to mark on the diameter face of the log where the cuts would go. While he was doing this I had made "ink." I took apart an old Ray-O-Vac battery and scooped out the black battery acid, which I mixed with a little water. After soaking a long string in this battery-acid ink, we wrapped it around the trunk and snapped it like a plumb line where we wanted to make the first cut. By this time it was too late to continue, so we went home.

The next day we continued the process. Manuel, with more knowledge, stood on top sawing backwards. I sawed forward and faced up at him. I had to be on my knees for the entire time because the tree was only four feet above my head as I knelt in the ditch. The diameter at the base of the log was almost as wide as the saw was long, so there were only six inches of play for each cut. It took all that day and half the next to get through the first section. We repeated this process for the other usable section of the log.

At this point the first section had to be cut into lumber small enough to transport. Each section was cut into planks that looked like oversized railroad ties. Again we marked where we would cut with our battery ink. To get the maximum amount of wood, we made the planks in a variety of cuts, mostly 10-, 12-, and 16-inches square. The sawmill would make these into finished planks. We had cut off slabs of bark to get squared piece of lumber. We worked three trees. Two were down and one had to be felled.

Manuel and I spent three more months getting all the good lumber from these logs. By the time we were finished, we had processed 11,500 board feet of lumber. Manuel had been told that the truck that would meet us down river would only handle our load if we had at least 10,000 board feet, and we cut extra in case there were any pieces lost in the river or rejected because of cracks or imperfections.

We were already starting to make plans for spending our money. We knew we were to be paid in lempiras, which at the time were two for one U.S. dollar. The rate we would be paid had been set at .85 lempiras for each board foot, so we figured we stood to make 850 lempiras ($425) to be split between the two of us, as we would only get paid for the 10,000 board feet.

The two teams finished cutting the lumber at about the same time, so we decided to work together to get it to the river's edge. Each team used a different color to mark its own lumber so there would be no confusion as to which lumber was whose.

We began moving the lumber on a Monday morning. The most difficult part was the first thirty feet, because we had to climb up the hill. We used the same technique as for carrying a casket. We slung two branches at right angles underneath the logs, then each man took an end of a branch, so that each branch had two men, one on each side of the log. Each log weighed between nine hundred and a thousand pounds—that's about 250 pounds on each man's shoulders. We'd leave the log at the flat top of the hill and go back down to get another, until we had a stack. Going uphill the four of us could carry only about a hundred board feet of lumber at a time, so you can imagine how many trips we had to take to move the entire pile. At the beginning, my neck, back, and shoulders hurt very much. After a couple hours I felt as if my back wasn't my own as it was completely numb.

After that it was downhill for three blocks. I thought this would be easier, but I soon found out that it wasn't. We used the same five-foot branch to carry the log down to the river, but this time there were only two of us per log. Manuel and I tied the branch to one end of the log then scooped it up with our forearms, lifting only the front of the log. We dragged the log behind us, walking until the hill started sloping downward, then we had to run as the log bumped along behind us. We had to keep our mouths closed as our jaws were shaken so hard that we would have bitten off our tongues if we had tried to talk. My back and shoulders were already sore from carrying the monsters up the hill; now my forearms were red and swollen.

Manuel had us stack the lumber far enough away from the river's present bank to still be out of the water after a week of constant rain, which would raise the river over five feet. By the time we were finished with all three trees of lumber, the two of us had a pile of lumber at least 8 feet high and about 7 feet long.

But we weren't finished yet. Manuel and I crossed the river to where Cristobal and Arturo were working and helped them finish up their trees. When we started, the "river" was really only a mountain stream. It was not deep enough to float huge logs, so we had to wait until it had rained for about five days in a row. We kept checking the water level and, meanwhile, hunted with slingshots. It was frustrating because without a rifle I had to just stand there while deer jumped over my head.

BREAKING HOME TIES

We also husked dried corn from Manuel's corn plantation to take to market. This was a delightful timekiller, especially when compared to carrying the logs. We filled a mesh hemp hammock with husked corn and then sewed the two long sides together by weaving string along the edges. We left the hammock suspended between two trees. Later we put a plastic tarp under it and beat on the hammock "cocoon" with sticks until the corn kernels loosened and fell on the tarp, leaving only cobs in the hammock.

While we waited for the rains, we went fishing. I fondly remembered Tio Chente, my first fishing teacher in San Luis. I'd find a rock in a shallow stream and throw the net, which was about twelve feet in diameter, over the rock, "capturing" the rock in the middle of the net. Next I'd take a sturdy stick, lift the net at the base of the rock, and poke around in the water. The sleeping fish left their dark resting place and went into the net. I'd slowly pull the net up above the rock and have fish in the bag that the net had made. When I put my hand under the bag I could feel the fish jiggling and jumping.

It was much easier at night. I just threw the net into the water, pulled it up, and took out the fish. But though I could catch more fish at night, I preferred doing this during the day. During the night there were too many zancudos and I had to spend all my time hitting my back with my wet shirt to keep them from biting.

Another diversion involved a snake. It reminded me of my encounter with the barba amarilla when I first got to Honduras. Manuel and his neighbors had many hunting dogs. One gray, cloudy morning a couple of Manuel's neighbors and I took the dogs and walked for a couple of hours up into the mountains. We heard one of the dogs barking and ran to see what it had found. It was excitedly digging a hole. With my machete I cut a branch off a nearby tree, hacked one end into a point, and began digging. In about 20 minutes I pulled out an armadillo. This armadillo was average size, about 10 pounds. Here was some meat to add to our diet of beans and rice.

We continued our journey and within about five hours had caught seven armadillos. We continued walking upstream and soon heard the dogs again chasing some animal. From the sound of the barking, we knew that these animals were far off and were getting further away. I was already tired from carrying my share of the armadillos because the four of them together weighed about 50 pounds. I suggested that I wait at the stream with all the armadillos. My companions agreed and took off.

I sat on a rock listening drowsily to the dogs barking in the distance and to the gurgling water. I lay back and closed my eyes, continuing to hold my machete. In the mountains there were animals that might attack. I myself didn't see any big cats, but I had seen skins like Cristobal's, and they were not small animals.

Suddenly, I heard a rustling in the leaves. I turned around and saw a snake coming toward me. It looked just like the one I had previously outstared. I didn't move. I let it come closer until it was within range. I swung my machete and cut the snake into two parts. It had been twelve feet long, now it was one foot plus eleven feet.

My friends returned soon after. "That snake is a barba amarilla, a yellow beard, the most poisonous snake in Honduras!"

"I know. This is the second one I've seen in Honduras."

After a week of rain, the stream filled up and we could start moving the logs downriver. Before sunrise, we started

BREAKING HOME TIES

dumping the logs into the deepest part of the river. Umberto, Manuel's brother-in-law who had been helping when we needed him, joined the four of us—Cristobal, Arturo, Manuel, and I. He had been clear-cutting overgrown brush for a nearby farmer so the farmer could plant corn. We told him that if he helped us he could have a share of our profits. I thought that for every day he worked for us Manuel and I would pay him three lempiras.

While we original four continued moving lumber into the stream, Umberto started down the river with the first logs. About five o'clock, when we had guided the wood down the river for about two kilometers, we dragged the logs up on the banks and went home for dinner.

This first day I had to walk about four kilometers with only one shoe as I had lost the other in a big sinkhole. The river had natural dammed ponds with waterfalls dropping to whirlpools, and then another waterfall leading to another whirlpool and so on. We came to a pond about three blocks long and half a block wide. As it was toward the end of the day, to make it easier to swim with the big logs, I had set my shoes on top of one of the logs. I was about twelve feet away when some of the logs in the middle of the pond bumped into each other and my shoes fell. I swam over, dove down, and grabbed one of the shoes just before it reached the bottom. I didn't see the other shoe, so I came up for air and asked Manuel to hang onto my shoe.

I dove down three times to try to find the other shoe. Now the water was muddy so I couldn't see a thing and by then my teammates were about a block and a half downstream. I gave up looking and caught up with my buddies. My friends teased me, saying that it was only the first day and I had already lost one shoe.

A Salvadoran's Journey

When the five of us reached home that day, it was after seven and already dark. Now I didn't notice the pain in my neck and back so much, because I had splinters and thorns from the mud and brush in my left foot. Manuel gave me a pair of his old rubber shoes, but he wore size ten and I wore a seven, so everybody could recognize where I had stepped because I was wearing two different sizes. Besides, the rubber shoe was heavy and collected lots of mud. When this happened, my friends called me *"Fenomeno."*

The next day we arose at four o'clock, and as usual I helped Manuel's wife grind corn in a hand grinder. We had hot tortillas, red beans, and rice for breakfast, followed by a cup of coffee, and then Manuel's wife packed a lunch for us to take along.

As soon as the sky began to brighten, we dumped the logs back into the river and continued swimming them down river. Sometimes the river narrowed, making the current stronger, and the logs wouldn't go straight. They would bog up and we'd have to free them. Luckily, none of us got hurt. This was very dangerous, as we could have been crushed between the logs.

I especially enjoyed this part of the work. As this was my first time going down the river, I saw many beautiful views and spotted many different kinds of animals, including deer, tapir, four-foot-long iguanas, and monkeys with bushy white tails and sideburns.

As we continued down the river I grew more and more worried. The other four had done this job before, and they kept mentioning a spot where the river widened and where there were crocodiles. I had never seen one, but they cautioned me that it looked just like a log moving along with the river current. As I had no shoes or shirt on, just shorts, their stories made me very nervous and very alert

BREAKING HOME TIES

when we came to the deepest part of the river. But our fears proved to be for nothing, because we never saw a crocodile.

We floated the logs down-river for six more days. It took more than a week from start to finish. We took time to rest only while we ate lunch, and only one of us could eat at a time, so we could take no more than five or ten minutes. We would lash two sections of logs together and sit on them while we ate. When we finished eating, we would jump off so the next person could jump on and start eating.

In rotation, one of us would lead. He would walk on the shore ahead of the logs with our dry clothes and our lunch. When I took my turn I was all alone for about two blocks, ahead of everyone, and I didn't like spending the time with no one to talk to.

Imagine how tired we grew doing this from six o'clock in the morning to five o'clock at night: eleven hours of swimming, pushing logs, and treading water. Then we had to put on our dry clothes and trudge home for two or three more hours. And, of course, the closer we got to our delivery point the longer it took us to get home.

What I remember most clearly is the day before we reached our final destination. This part of the river passed through a flat valley, and up ahead we could see it beginning to wind. From a distance, the canyon we were about to enter looked amazingly beautiful, but it also looked mysterious and scary. For the equivalent of two or three blocks the river ran between two mountains with no beaches or banks on either side—only sharp, straight sides up the mountains. "Here," I thought, "is where the crocodiles would be if they are any place in the river at all." I was glad my suspicions proved to be unfounded.

After we passed safely through this canyon-like stretch, the lead man began guiding the first logs towards the shallows. Though it was already about two o'clock by the time we had pulled all the logs onto the bank, we still had to carry the logs up the bank fifteen or so yards. Manuel and I had brought down river a hundred logs and Arturo and Cristobal had about the same number. Again, going uphill it took four of us to carry each log, so we had to make 200 trips up this 15-foot embankment to pile up our logs. Luckily, mahogany is a very dense wood, so the huge logs floated well and did not get waterlogged. We didn't finish until 6:30, and it was after 11 p.m. when we reached home.

By 7:00 the following morning we were back by our logs waiting for the truck to arrive, which came about half an hour later.

Now we had to load the log blocks onto the truck. In our verbal contract with the truck owner we had agreed to do the loading ourselves so we could avoid the expense of hiring loaders. The driver had to be paid to take the logs to the mill, and we didn't want any other expenses we could avoid. We gave the driver a list of the various sizes of our lumber and told him about our system of coding the wood with different colors, and while Umberto watched he kept track of the amounts we loaded on the truck.

Finally, at about two o'clock, the logs were all loaded. The driver walked around the truck, inspecting the load, and said, "Everything looks good. Let's see, today's Thursday, and I'm taking the lumber to be sold in San Pedro Sula now. (I knew is was more than an eight-hour drive and that he would arrive in San Pedro on Friday.) You guys come over to my house on Sunday and I'll have your money for you." We shook hands all around.

During the long walk home I again made plans as to what I would do with my share. I thought, "Ten thousand cubic feet at $.85 per cubic foot. Manuel and I will split the 8,500 lempiras (not the 850 lempiras I thought at first), so I'll get 4,250 lempiras!" That was the equivalent of $2,125 in U.S. money, which was a huge amount of money, more than I had ever had at one time.

I was excited, picturing myself with all that money. I thought, "First I'll buy the rifle and then go back for those hunting dogs."

I had been eyeing a young puppy, a purebred track hound pointer that was considered to be the best hunting breed in Central America. The owner was asking 200 lempiras for it. I had had dogs before and had taken good care of them, training them to hunt iguanas, rabbits, armadillos, squirrels, and Cornish hens. In El Salvador, nobody bought or sold dogs because there were too many in the street, but those were all mixed breeds. My dream was to own a purebred hunting dog.

The man who was selling the dog was also selling a horse. He was asking 250 lempiras, but because I was interested in buying the dog he offered to sell me the horse for only 200 lempiras. I had agreed, and had asked him if he would keep them until I settled in a little on my newly built place.

Next my mind flashed to the land I had picked out, where I wanted to build a little house. The land was free as long as no one had claimed it. I had already spent a whole day marking out the borders of the property, which was trapezoidal, with a stream forking at one edge. The house would be a simple log cabin and wouldn't cost me much, as the building materials were right there on the land. "I'll even hire a couple of people to help me build it," I thought. "That would be only cost me about thirty lempiras, and I'll bet we could finish it in a week."

I realized that I would have it made. "I'll be a landowner!" I chuckled to myself.

With some of the money, I needed to buy corn, beans, rice, and sesame seeds to plant, all crops that did well in this environment and that I would be able to sell. On the side, I'd have a patch of yucca, a starchy vegetable in the potato family, which grew wild all around. I was also planning to buy a couple of piglets, some chickens, and a rooster, as they were all very cheap. "And," I thought, "I'll still have enough money to buy kitchen utensils and a radio, and even save some money for an emergency."

At this moment all my dreams seemed to be within my reach. I could almost touch them.

Sunday afternoon we were at Manuel's house, happy and joking, waiting for Arturo and Manuel to return from Bonito Oriental where the truck driver lived. When I spotted Arturo and Manuel, I could tell from half a block away that something had gone wrong.

We listened impatiently while Manuel told us what had happened.

"The truck driver could not sell our lumber because the mill owner said the quality is too poor," Manuel said. "The driver, deciding that it was impossible to sell it anywhere to anybody, unloaded the logs someplace in San Pedro Sula. He said he needed to empty his truck so he could carry cement back to Bonito Oriental. He asked us if we wanted our lumber brought back to Oriental. He told me that he would help us go back and get it, but he said it would cost us another 400 lempiras."

Cristobal, who was standing next to a big tree outside Manuel's house, turned and swung his machete into the tree. "*Que hijo de la gran puta!*" "Sonofabitch!"

BREAKING HOME TIES

I felt cheated. I was rabid. "There is no god," I yelled. "What are we going to do?" I asked the others.

There was no answer to my question.

Arturo jumped up from his hunkered-down position and screamed, "Let's chop his head off!"

The idea raced through my mind to burn up the driver's truck. I also thought about putting sugar in his diesel tank.

We were so disgusted that we all agreed that we would not go to San Pedro Sula to get the lumber. "We've worked long enough! We don't want to continue working for free for that motherfucker!"

Umberto looked at our faces. He said, "Doing what we did, we could have filled a barrel with our sweat. And as pay for our work we didn't even get a bottle of whiskey to drown our sorrows for just one moment."

11

Niños

After Arturo and Manuel had finished telling us about the money, I said, "I'm leaving tomorrow morning."

They tried to get me to change my mind. "We can continue working and find a different driver."

I could not be civil. All I could do was hurl insults at them. After being cheated out of almost four months of hard labor, I blamed everyone.

I was too mad to fall asleep. The same thoughts raced over and over through my mind. My initial anger had been with the truck driver. But then almost immediately I grew suspicious of everyone. "Are Manuel and Arturo telling the truth? Maybe they and Cristobal cut a deal with the truck driver and had him sell the lumber and split the money only with them. Umberto helped us only a little, and maybe Manuel and Arturo felt justified in cutting him out of his share. But I shouldn't have been cut out. I was a full partner! I worked more than three months with those guys, damn it!"

"I wish the truck driver was here, then I'd be able to find out the truth before I kill him!"

I thought about confronting Manuel and Arturo, but I realized that if I provoked them I might get myself killed. "That would finish my life, my anger, and my worries all at the same time!" I raged. "What am I going to do with my life? Here I am 27 years old and I still don't have a home, a family, or a country I can be safe in!"

BREAKING HOME TIES

By five o'clock I had made up my mind that I had better leave. I knew I could go back to Doña Carmen's for a while. I didn't really want to go there, as I knew it would never be my home, but I knew I had to get away from this mountain.

I got up and gathered together the little bit of stuff I owned—my machete, my backpack, and a small radio/cassette tape player.

Manuel's wife was already up making coffee and grinding corn for tortillas. She pleaded with me not to leave until after I had eaten breakfast.

"Thanks very much, but I have given enough trouble here. I apologize for everything and for not paying for all the meals you have given me. I should have been paid. Because I have not been paid, you can see that I can't pay you as I have nothing."

She said, "The coffee is almost boiling. Wait a minute and you can have a cup before you leave."

"Thanks anyway, I've got to start walking. I've got a long way to go."

I stepped out the doorway and called back over my shoulder, "Goodbye everybody and thanks for having me here."

I heard Manuel and Umberto saying goodbye from their beds.

I started towards Bonito Orientale, walking fast because I was so angry. I was still muttering the same sentences over and over to myself.

When I was about two kilometers away, nearing a river crossing, I thought I heard someone yelling my name. I looked back and listened for a few seconds. I didn't hear anything, so I started across. When I was almost to the other side, I again heard, "Riiii-carrrr-do." Once on the other side, I sat down on a big rock. From behind a small embankment and some bushes, I finally spotted someone walking toward me from the direction I had come. When he got to a clearing in the river, I recognized Umberto.

I watched him ford the river. When he had caught his breath enough to talk, he said, "Now you have a partner for your journey. When you said goodbye, I started thinking about my future. That's when I got up, grabbed my clothes and my machete, and started running to catch up with you."

Though I knew he too was without money, I was glad not to have to travel alone.

We got up and continued walking, talking as we went. We talked about difficult experiences and situations, mainly about how we would live and survive. But we tried to avoid talking about what had just happened to us.

Umberto told me how he had come to be in Honduras instead of being with his family in El Salvador.

"I was a partner with my brother-in-law. We had a still in the mountains to make *chaparro.*" Chaparro is a popular corn-based moonshine. "One afternoon after we had been processing and drinking up part of the profits, we were about a block away from our house. We started having a playful skirmish with our machetes, and he swung his machete so quickly that he cut my right hand. I grabbed my machete in my left hand and started defending myself for real, because he kept coming at me, even though he saw my hand bleeding badly. I heard my sister and my five nieces and nephews screaming at us. *'Paren, paren no peleen!'* "Stop! Stop! Don't fight!'"

"We were both very drunk and my brother-in-law fell down. I lost my control and started chopping on him over and over.

BREAKING HOME TIES

"My sister and her kids rushed towards me. I came to my senses and looked down at what I had done. I looked at my sister and her orphaned children and ran away. I kept running until I got to Honduras."

He told me that even though he knew his sister and her children would never forgive him for what he had done, he felt he must continue to help them. He said that the oldest child at the time of the killing was six or seven years old and the youngest was a six-month-old.

Umberto said, "I have been living as a fugitive here in Honduras for two years. I can't make enough money here to meet my obligations to my sister. I am just barely able to take care of myself in this place."

I told him how I myself had come to be in Honduras, but as I talked my difficulties and disappointments didn't seem so bad compared to del Cid's.

We continued walking all day towards Bonito Oriental, talking off and on. That night we had to get off the road to find a place to sleep. We chose a space under an African palm tree growing in an orchard, the only trees on this flat land. They were imported (though none were ever imported to El Salvador) some time ago by the conquistadors to be grown for their palm oil.

For four more days we continued traveling to get to Doña Carmen's. We didn't even have the money for bus fare so, sometimes we thumbed short rides, sometimes we were lucky enough to catch a longer one.

Doña Carmen gave us jobs cutting sugarcane, which was now in season. We carried the raw canes on horseback to the processing plant, where they were turned into *dulce de atado*, a cone-shaped candy made from the raw sugarcane.

A Salvadoran's Journey

This sugarcane-cutting season in Honduras is special in my memory for another reason. One day, Umberto and I returned from the fields sweaty and tired, and I was kind of down as we came near Doña Carmen's house. But I cheered up instantly because I spotted my uncle Mauricio sitting in front of the main door talking with some of Doña Carmen's family.

"Buenes tardes," I said to everyone there. *"Bendito, Tio!"* How are you, Uncle?"

"How have you been? Haven't seen you for a long time," Mauricio replied. "Your cousin Bartolo and his friend, Roberto Lobo, are here with me. They're in the orchard behind the house."

Bartolo had finished the sixth grade in San Luis about five years ahead of me. He went to high school in Ciudad Barrios, and then joined the National Guard. He stayed in the Guard for six years. Bartolo had a drinking problem and was asked to leave the National Guard in 1974.

He married a teacher from the countryside and had two boys. Bartolo supported his family as a tailor. As the situation in our country worsened in 1978 and 1979, my cousin drank more and more and stayed out till all hours of the night.

I remember my aunt, Uncle Mauricio's wife, following Bartolo around with a flashlight at night. My primo had a bad temper and knew how to use firearms from his National Guard experience. Many friends of his were being "disappeared." Bartolo could get drunk and start fighting at any time and his family didn't want him to disappear. So, Uncle Mauricio brought him to Honduras, hoping his drinking problem would go away and that he would stay alive if he left El Salvador.

BREAKING HOME TIES

I had only talked with Uncle Mauricio for a few minutes, but I was so eager to see Bartolo that I couldn't wait. "Please excuse me, everyone. I want to see my cousin and his friend."

I hung up my machete and my *calabazo* (a gourd for carrying water) on a nail on the side of the house and ran to the orchard. It was easy to find them as they were noisily talking with some of the other men workers. Some of the guys were up in one of the trees tossing oranges down to those on the ground.

I was so glad to see my cousin and his friend that, as I shook Bartolo's hand, I blurted out, "What the hell are you doing here?"

"We're on our way north," they said in unison.

"But why did you start by coming here, south of El Salvador? You should have gone to Guatemala."

"First, we have to get documentation—not only for ourselves, but for three *niños* (kids)." I looked around for three young boys, but didn't see anyone. "Here in Honduras it's easy to get those papers and also to get a tourist visa to Mexico."

"How long will you be able to stay? How long will it take you to gather everything you need?" I was anxious for them to stay. I wanted them to stay longer than a couple of days. I didn't want to have to say another goodbye.

Bartolo replied, "They told us it could be a week or two."

"I'm glad I'll have your company while you're here."

Just then we were called into dinner. The three boys were already at the table. I guessed that they were between eight and twelve years old. I was curious why they were here. I whispered to Bartolo, "Who are these kids? Where are their parents?"

A Salvadoran's Journey

"Their parents are already in the United States, waiting for the kids. Roberto and I are taking them to their folks."

While Doña Carmen blessed the food, I peeked again at the boys. They looked rather sad. They seemed already to be missing El Salvador and their grandparents and aunts. The oldest—I later learned his name was Juanito —looked pretty pale because he had been carsick on the bus from Santa Lucia, throwing up continuously for two days.

After dinner Bartolo and I went outside on the patio to talk. Bartolo updated me on the status of our mutual friends back in El Salvador. "Though these boys are probably safe because they are so young—Juanito is twelve, Saul is ten, and Basilio, eight—the situation at home is very dangerous," he said. "The National Guard is getting more aggressive all the time. They have killed some men in our town, even some women. You do know your friend, Raton, was killed shortly after you left, don't you?"

Later Bartolo, Uncle Mauricio, Roberto Lobo, and the three boys went to a nearby town with "borrowed" birth certificates. All of them got new ID with their pictures and new names. A couple days later, they went to Tegucigalpa, the capital, and used these ID cards to obtain Honduran passports and visas to Mexico.

On our way back to Bonito Oriental, Umberto and I had agreed to become partners. We worked together getting contracts from the village residents to weed and plant their land. On the municipal land the people in the village could all share the planting and the harvest. For a week after Umberto and I became partners, we helped put up the fence around the community plot. For that help we became members of the co-op. They told us we could have this piece of land and all we had to do was clear it, plow, and plant. We just supplied the seeds. We intended to plant

BREAKING HOME TIES

beans and corn in our block-square plot. During the two weeks the boys were at Doña Carmen's, we spent time planting the way we had planned.

One afternoon when I returned from planting, I was sitting on the patio talking with Bartolo, and he made a surprising suggestion.

"Why don't you go north with us," he said. "There's no future for you here in Honduras."

I was thinking to myself, "There is no future for me at Dona Carmen's. But what I said was, "I'm broke and I don't see any possibility of going north with you all."

In a way, I liked this place. I liked the friendly people, and I felt close enough so that I might someday be able return to El Salvador. But I didn't share these feelings with my cousin because he had just left a scary time in El Salvador.

Later that afternoon Bartolo again approached me, this time bringing my uncle along.

Uncle Mauricio explained, "I plan to go only as far as Mexico City, D.F. *(Districto Federal)*, with Bartolo, Roberto, and the niños. I don't want to go any farther. I'd like you to go with them so each of you has only one boy to take care of."

Again I explained that I didn't have enough money to make the trip, adding that I had some obligations to my partner Umberto.

"Talk it over with your partner. You'll need ID and a passport."

I now realized that my uncle was really giving me an order, and I had been brought up by my grandmother to do what I was told to do by my elders, especially family.

"I only can get enough money for my ID and a passport," I replied.

A Salvadoran's Journey

"Bartolo has money and he will help you as much as he can."

I thought back over the past two or three months. Until I had been cheated out of my share of the lumber proceeds, I had been certain that I would stay in Honduras. Then when I got back to Doña Carmen's I decided this wouldn't be such a bad place to live while I was waiting to return to El Salvador. But now that I had the opportunity to go north, I realized that I had been defeated and that I had simply given up, letting circumstances rule my fate.

That same night I told Umberto what was going on. He said that he would go with us if it were possible, but that he knew he had no chance of going. "You should go, Ricardo. If you want, we can sell our plot. It's already planted."

"Why don't you buy my half so you can keep what we've worked for?" I suggested.

He looked directly at me and said, "I don't have the money to buy your half. If we can sell the whole thing you can get at least 100 lempiras for your share, and all of my savings only amounts to 60 lempiras."

"That's enough for me. Keep all the land and give me the 60 lempiras." It made me feel better that he would be able to keep what we had worked for.

I asked him if he would allow me to take his birth certificate, even though he was 8 years older than I was at the time and it might be difficult to look 35 when I was only 27! But my cousin and Roberto Lobo were both 32, so I thought maybe we could all pass for the same age.

A few days later, I thought to myself, "What is waiting for me up ahead?" I had my ID, a passport, and a visa, and even had 85 lempiras in my pocket, yet I had no idea how these would change my life.

1 2

The Journey North

From Aldea Casitas where Doña Carmen lived, we took a bus north to San Pedro Sula, the largest city in Honduras. We were seven in all—Juanito, Saul, and Basilio, Tio Mauricio, Bartolo, Roberto Lobo and I. Three kids, four adults.

From the bus terminal we walked to the closest *hospedaje,* sort of like a roadside motel, lodging, where we rented a couple rooms. We left all of our things there and then went out to explore the center of town. We didn't want to be robbed or appear to be foreigners in San Pedro. After a leisurely walk, we returned to the hospedaje, rested some, then went out again for dinner.

During the afternoon we saw many beggars—in the streets, on street corners, everywhere. But when we went out for dinner the beggars had disappeared and now all we saw were women. By their dress, their makeup, and their shouts to men, we knew they were prostitutes. They stood in groups of three or four, wearing miniskirts and holding cigarettes in their hands.

Bartolo teased me, saying that they were calling for me.

It is a sad fact that most of the women were black. This was my third time in San Pedro Sula, as I had traveled through the city on my way to and from Manuel's. But this was the first time for the rest of our group and they were all staring at the black-skinned women. As in other countries on the Atlantic coast, black people had been brought as

BREAKING HOME TIES

slaves from Africa to Honduras. We had never seen black women in El Salvador. The only people with black skin that we had seen in El Salvador were Brazilian soccer players.

"Close your mouths and pretend you don't see anything unusual," I said.

Returning to our hospedaje after dinner, we sent the boys to bed, then stood outside making plans for the following morning. We decided we needed to be up by 5 o'clock so we could catch the first bus to Guatemala at 6 a.m. Tio Mauricio repeated his wish that I take his place as one of the adults in the three-adults, three-children plan. He said he would see us to the bus then return to El Salvador.

Getting on the bus went as we had planned. But we didn't get to Guatemala as soon as we had thought because of an unexpected problem: we were trying to cross the border with minors who had different last names from us adults. Since this was all new to us, we didn't realize until this point that we should have obtained written authorization from the parents to travel with the boys to the United States. Had we known, we would have forged the documents. Fortunately, we were able to solve the problem by bribing the person in charge.

Once this two-hour ordeal was over, we walked the two blocks from the customs/immigration house to catch a minibus for the 10-minute ride to Esquipulas, Guatemala, where we would stay the night.

I had never been to Esquipulas before, but I had certainly had heard about it. Santos, my Aunt Juana's husband, who had also been my boss in San Luis de la Reina, frequently had taken truckloads of paying passengers to Esquipulas for pilgrimages.

A Salvadoran's Journey

Many people throughout Central America believed that the *Cristo Negro* (the black statue of Jesus in the cathedral) at Esquipulas had performed miracles for them. The pilgrims would come to ask for something, usually related to healing an illness or other physical condition. They would make a pledge, promising to return to fulfill the pledge. One woman I had heard of had traveled from San Luis to Esquipulas, a 13- or 14-hour drive, asking that her hand be healed of its swelling. She pledged to bring back a silver hand if her hand was cured. This woman's deathbed wish 20 years later was for one of her sisters to take a silver charm of a right hand and give it to the Cristo Negro de Esquipulas.

It was about 2:30 when we rented rooms across the park from the cathedral. At that time one of the cheapest places in the town was near the cathedral. Despite our tiredness from traveling all day and from the anxiety about getting the boys across the border, we were eager to see the cathedral. We didn't even eat first, but all went across the street and entered the cathedral.

Maybe because I had heard so much all my life about this place, I was unprepared for what I saw. Now that I was actually standing there I was disappointed, as my expectations hadn't been met. I thought the cathedral would be bigger, more European looking. I thought the statue itself would be the size of a human, but it was only three and a half feet tall!

Even though we hadn't planned to come here as pilgrims, I suddenly realized that I did have a wish, a request. "God, I pray to you to keep us safe and alive and allow us to return here one day under other circumstances."

BREAKING HOME TIES

After leaving the cathedral, we went back to our rooms and slept all the rest of the afternoon. At 3:00 the following morning, we got up and went to the front of our hospedage to wait for the bus going north.

The bus trip proved to be yet another ordeal. Several times the bus was stopped by the army, and everyone had to get off and show identification papers. I felt as if I was back in El Salvador because of the army's harassment. Guatemala had been in a state of war for a long time. I supposed the army was looking for weapons, but I was still afraid that one of them could stop and say to one of us "You stay here." No reason, no cause.

The kids were scared and shaking each time this happened. Juanito continued to vomit, and even when his stomach was empty, he had the dry heaves and was sweating. While trying to take care of him, I was attempting to look relaxed so I would not draw attention to ourselves. We just did what the soldiers told us to do. When asked, we said we were going to see relatives in Mexico. I don't know if they believed us or didn't care if we were telling the truth or not.

None of us had been in Guatemala before. We had to deal each moment with what we were handed. Trouble with immigration one day, army harassment the next.

We reached Guatemala City at about noon that day. We didn't look around the city; we just got off one bus and got on another in the bus terminal. At about 4:30 p.m. we arrived at the Mexican-Guatemalan border town of Talisman. Whenever vendors came through the bus with food, we ate.

We got off the bus with our backpacks and immediately went to stand in line to pass through the Guatemalan emigration offices, which, for a change, proved to be easy.

A Salvadoran's Journey

At the Mexican offices, we ran into a problem, however. An official asked for our passports and visas to Mexico and asked us how much money we were carrying. We told him we had $400 for the six of us. Bartolo had U.S. dollars. I had changed my lempiras into Guatemalan *quetzales* at the border the day before, as I no longer needed Honduran money. (At that time 70 Honduran lempiras equaled about 35 quetzales, which were about equivalent to one U.S. dollar. I had changed only enough lempiras into quetzales to get us through Guatemala.)

He said, "Each of you adults must have a minimum of $200 apiece to be considered tourists. Your visas are tourist visas, and tourists travel to other countries to spend money there. You obviously are not coming to our country to be a tourist, so I can't let you in to Mexico."

We three adults talked quietly amongst ourselves. At first I didn't say anything. Then I said to the others, "Go ahead. You two can take the money and go if you want to." But they said they wanted to stay together, according to our original plan, so all six of us walked back to the Guatemala border. The more obstacles we had to deal with, the more convinced I was that going on was becoming just a huge hassle that I didn't need.

We walked dejectedly back toward the bus we had come on, not knowing what to do next. When we got near the border, we spotted another bus. The cobrador in charge of collecting the money for those bus tickets was shouting, "La frontera, Tecun Uman. Tecun Uman." We were at one *frontera*—one border crossing, at Talisman—and I suddenly realized there was another one at Tecun Uman. "This place will not let us enter Mexico, but maybe the other place will," I explained to the others. We asked the

BREAKING HOME TIES

cobrador how far it was to Tecun Uman and learned that it was just 30 minutes away.

It was about 6 p.m. by the time we arrived in Tecun Uman. There we talked with another cobrador, one who was about our age. We explained why we were going to the other border, and he offered to help. We also told him that we were hungry, and gave him some money to buy us food.

"First," he said, "I will drop you off at a room, which you will have to pay for, then I will go and get you the food and make arrangements for you to cross the border later tonight."

When he came back he told us that he knew one of the border police who began work at midnight, but that there was a catch. "Each of you six must pay twenty U.S. dollars! In this situation, no lempiras, no quetzales!"

While he was gone, we argued about the cost. We had the money, but did we want to give up $120 that easily? No, we didn't. We decided we could do it for less, so we made a deal with the cobrador.

At midnight the boys and I went to the Mexican immigration office with our passports in hand, each passport containing $20. The office was deserted at that hour, except for one official. We gave the passports to the officer, who stamped them and waved us through. The boys and I walked the five or six blocks to where we had arranged to meet Bartolo and Roberto, where we were all going to spend the rest of the night.

Meanwhile, Bartolo and Roberto, who had not wanted to pay $20 each, had worked out a separate plan with the cobrador. He would take them to the river that divides Guatemala and Mexico. At a small house next to the river they would rent three inner tubes. For $5 each, Bartolo and Roberto were going to float and paddle across the river to the Mexico side. The cobrador would serve as their guide and then take them to the hotel where we would be waiting.

The room at the hotel where we were to wait had not been reserved in my name, so the boys and I had to wait outside on the street. The boys were so tired they would lie down on the ground and fall asleep. But we had to look like we belonged there, so every time I saw a police patrol or a night watchman with a whistle in his hand, which they blew every ten minutes, I had to wake the boys, pulling them by their shirts to a standing position. We'd continue walking as if we were going some place. Wherever there was a truck where we could hide, we did, but the streets were deserted so it was easy to spot us. All this time we had were carrying the luggage for all six of us.

Finally, after waiting for about two hours, which felt more like two weeks, we heard someone whistle and spotted the cobrador, Roberto, and Bartolo about two blocks away walking towards us. When they came closer, we saw they were soaking wet.

I was pretty upset because we had been waiting in the street for so long. I yelled at them, "Why are you so late?"

"We got caught on the other side of the river."

They explained that when Roberto and Bartolo had gotten caught on the Mexican shore, the immigration official picked them up as soon as they climbed ashore, and wanted another $40, $20 each for his pocket.

But Bartolo had balked. "No," he had said. "You get our passports stamped and bring them back to us. Then we'll give you the $40."

Bartolo and Roberto felt that they had been set up by the cobrador. They realized that silence was their ally then, because the men could have taken all their money, as well as their lives.

BREAKING HOME TIES

By that time it was about 3 a.m., so we all went to the room and fell instantly asleep. But it was a very short sleep for such a long day because, even though we were exhausted, we had to be up by 6 o'clock to catch the bus to Mexico City.

Although Mexico City was a place where all of us thought we could feel a little more stable, we were still pretty tense. In the bus depot we saw some people asking for identification, but each of us adults took one child and avoided looking any officials in the eye, so we were able to get on the bus without being stopped.

Once we were on the bus, we grew more anxious as the bus stopped every 15 to 20 minutes to allow a guard or other official to get on the bus to check everyone's papers. Mostly, they were looking for illegal aliens headed north who were coming from Central American countries. We decided that they weren't following orders as part of an official policy, that they were doing it just because they wanted to put money in their own pockets. Now we were glad that Roberto and Bartolo had been caught crossing the river, as otherwise, we would not all have had visas and stamped passports. Now, we thought, "Nobody can stop us or take any more money from us. We are all "legal" in Mexico!"

13

At Home in Mexico

It took us two days to reach to Mexico City, most of the ride through boring desert-like country. Saul and Basilio did fine, but Juanito was motion sick again, vomiting often and the rest of the time sweating and looking very pale and weak. Even though Bartolo and Roberto Lobo now had visas to be in Mexico, we were constantly concerned about the rest of us when the bus was stopped and searched. My thoughts were constantly on El Salvador and my family, wishing I could go back, but wondering what lay ahead for me and for the others.

We were all glad to reach the city, but we still had a long way to go. When Tio Mauricio had brought the boys to Doña Carmen's, he had given us instructions on how to get to where Natan and Conce were staying. He told us that the lady of the house had been to the U.S. and had met Conce's mother, who had called Tio Mauricio after the señora returned to Mexico.

I was looking forward to seeing Conce and Natan again. Since we had spent Christmas Eve together at Doña Carmen's, I felt a million years had passed, even though it was only five months. I had lived in many different places, doing different jobs, earning money in strange currencies, and here I was traveling to yet another unfamiliar place. I was so happy that I would be able to catch up with them for a moment to find out how they were doing and how it felt to be in Mexico.

BREAKING HOME TIES

At the bus terminal the six of us boarded the bus for Colima, which turned out to be a city of about a million people located close to the western coast. Juanito was still sick, but feeling a little better.

We found the house easily and had a joyful reunion. Natan was working as a truck driver, delivering produce in the city as well as to nearby villages. He said he was happy with his job and the people he worked for. Conce was working in construction with Henrique and Camillo. Lana, Camillo's wife had returned to El Salvador with her parents.

For four days the six of us became tourists, with Conce as our guide as he took a leave without pay from his job. We walked everywhere, going to parks and downtown. The four days we spent there went by very quickly and I didn't feel so alone. Even though we were having a wonderful time, we felt very crowded, as we were staying with a family of seven people in a very small house. With us ten extras, that meant finding places for seventeen of us to sleep. Nevertheless, this short break in my nomadic life was a happy one because I was together with so many friends and family from El Salvador.

After these four days, it was time to continue our journey north. From Colima we took a bus to Guadalajara. When we got off the bus, each of us adults took one of the boys by the hand. We had heard that this city was very dangerous for travelers, and we didn't want to spend any more time in it than necessary. We walked toward the street, away from the crowded terminal. I walked in front with Basilio, the 10-year-old.

"Where is the train terminal?" I asked a passerby.

"Continue straight about five blocks and you will see it on the left side of the street."

A Salvadoran's Journey

We found it easily and learned that the train was scheduled to leave in the afternoon of the next day. We had spotted a pension about a block before the station so we went back and spent the night there. In the morning we had to check out of the pension several hours before we needed to be at the station, so we had to walk around with our backpacks on. The boys didn't like walking around with their packs, but I told them we didn't want any questions from policemen. Our visas said we were going to be in Mexico City, and we didn't want anyone to notice that now we were going north out of the city looking like travelers.

To be even less obvious, we split into three groups, but someone always had his eye out for the others. One pair at a time, we went into the station to buy our tickets. When we boarded the train, we saw many policemen around. I don't know how Bartolo and Roberto felt, but I felt like an outlaw of sorts.

We were on the train for two more days. We were heading for a little town outside Los Mochis, which is located on the western coast of Mexico in the state of Sinaloa. When we finally arrived, at 11 o'clock at night, I showed the address we had to a passerby and asked for directions to San Ignacio.

"That's about an hour away from the center of town. You need to catch a bus to downtown Los Mochis and from there catch another bus to the place you want. But the buses run only during the day."

"Is there a good place to spend the night?" I asked.

"The closest place is 10 minutes away by car, but many travelers sleep on the sidewalk outside this terminal."

I was grateful to the man for giving me so much information, and thanked him very much, then returned to the other five.

BREAKING HOME TIES

As soon as I had finished telling everyone what I had learned, the boys started running around gathering newspapers from trashcans. They were excited that they could be helpful. I wasn't excited, just very tired, but I couldn't repress a smile while I gathered up newspapers for my own "mattress." Though I felt a sense of shared responsibility with Roberto and Bartolo, I realized that I had bonded with the kids as if they were my own nephews or younger brothers. Though Juan, was the oldest, he had proven to be shy and cautious, in addition to being scared and homesick. Saul, the eight-year-old, was the baby and had almost forgotten his parents. Basilio, now ten years old, was the impatient one. He knew we were going to see his parents and was anxious to get there. Like most kids he had no concept of distance and kept asking, "When will we see our parents? Are we almost there?" And like any parent, I kept saying, "We are about half way there."

But I didn't reflect for too long. We were all so tired that as soon as we hit our newspaper mattresses we fell asleep as if we were dead.

The next morning we awoke early and caught the bus to downtown. Even though I was concentrating so hard on getting the boys delivered safely, I had time to look around a little. Los Mochis is located on very flat land, and unlike Mexico City, where there are many tall skyscrapers, the tallest buildings at this time were only three stories tall. Los Mochis is also a busy commercial city, so the bus terminal was crowded and there were many people on the streets. Vendors on the streets were selling everything imaginable. We had a nice breakfast of fried beans, cheese, tortillas, scrambled eggs, and coffee in the bus terminal. I hadn't eaten this well since we left Honduras.

A Salvadoran's Journey

After we had finished eating, I asked the waitress where I could catch the bus to San Ignacio and learned we would have to wait another two hours. While waiting we mingled with the people walking around in the terminal. As soon as we saw the bus parking, we went to stand in line for it. The waitress had told us that it would leave at 8:30, whether the bus was full or not.

I sat by the window enjoying the view. The flat land and the low buildings meant that there were great views everywhere of the city. As soon as we left the city limits, I saw how well irrigated the land was. Channels of water flowed everywhere. Many different crops were being grown—cotton, tomatoes, sesame seeds, carrots, corn, and many other vegetables. I had good feelings about the place, guessing that this was a place where many people were able to find work. I thought maybe this might be a good place to return to once I had delivered the boys to their parents.

It took only half an hour to reach our destination, a small town called Cortinas, near the village of San Ignacio. To get there, the bus turned off the main highway and onto a dusty dirt road. On the way there, we passed a couple of small *ejidos*, small pleasant-looking villages that appealed to me. Each ejido had its own little school, with a lot of kids playing happily in the schoolyard. So far I liked what I had seen of this part of Mexico. But there was one thing I was not seeing—trees. I really missed our Salvadoran trees.

We were looking for the Sylvester Vegas family, so I asked the cobrador if he knew a family by this name.

"Of course I know them," he said. "Everyone knows them. One of the Vegas brothers is the sheriff of St. Ignacio."

My heart sank. I felt as if I was about to enter the lion's mouth. Then I quickly realized that the boys' father might be a friend of the sheriff. "If that is the case, we might be in good hands," I thought.

The cobrador pointed out the Vegas' house, and the bus dropped us about two blocks away. Bartolo was in charge of the kids, so he had to walk up to the door and ask for Sr. Vegas. Roberto Lobo and I stood in front of the house on the street holding our charges' hands. This Vegas house proved to be a small temporary-looking structure of sticks and cardboard. One could see all the way through the house to the back yard. The only thing permanent-looking about the place was the tile roof.

Señor and Señora Vegas came out to welcome us and soon asked if we were hungry.

"Thank you, no. We had breakfast in Los Mochis," I spoke up. "The boys' father gave us your address and said you could help us," Bartolo informed them.

"I would be glad to help. I have already promised him I'd do anything I could," Sr. Vargas added.

Sr. Vegas invited us into the back yard, where there were chairs and hammocks in the shade. It was beginning to get very hot, so one of his older children went to the store and got sodas for all of us.

After we had exchanged news and gotten better acquainted, Sylvester Vegas took us to meet his parents, who lived on the other side of the back yard. Their house was bigger and more permanent, with separated bedrooms and a kitchen next to the corrals. Sylvester's parents appeared to be about 75 or 80 years old.

Sylvester asked, "Would it be okay for some of these fellows to sleep here?"

Don Tacho Vegas, his father, said, "That's no problem. They can all stay here together if they want."

A Salvadoran's Journey

"I will work for you in exchange for your hospitality," I said.

"Do any of you have any technical skills?" he asked.

We told them that Bartolo was a tailor and knew how to sew pants and that Roberto and I had grown up working in agriculture and taking care of cattle. "We appreciate your trust," I added. "You will not be disappointed in us."

As we were talking, I watched a tall man in his thirties walking towards us from a house nearby. He looked like a TV cowboy, with a gun in its holster and a gun belt full of bullets. I looked up and saw a silver star on this man's chest. I suddenly remembered what the bus worker had said about the sheriff in the family.

I must have looked worried because before the man could get close enough to overhear, Sylvester whispered, "He's my brother."

Sylvester said to his brother, "You see these three kids? These are three of the children of the couple I lived with in the state of Washington. That family was very nice to me, and I will do anything I can to help these people get to Washington State."

"Where are they from?" the sheriff asked.

"They are from El Salvador. As you know, the situation there is very dangerous. They escaped first to Honduras, where they got Honduran papers and visas to come to Mexico." Sylvester talked to him as a brother, not as the sheriff. I liked the way he made us feel as if we too were part of the family.

"How long are they planning to stay in San Ignacio?"

"They don't know yet," Sylvester said, "but I will communicate tomorrow with the people in Washington State and, hopefully, we'll put everything together so they can continue their trip north soon."

143

BREAKING HOME TIES

I waited for the conversation to pause, then asked the sheriff, "Is there any kind of work to do here, so I can use my time well while I am here?"

"Of course. There's always plenty to do in this place. I myself am starting to harvest sesame seeds tomorrow. If any of you want to come work, wait outside in the street tomorrow at 7:30 a.m. and I will drive by and pick you up."

"I will be waiting for you." Now I seemed to be talking to this man, who was a brother, the sheriff, and now my future *jefe* (boss).

I was pleased. I felt that maybe I had opened a little gap and was establishing a place for myself as part of the family. I was eager to help in any way I could. I suddenly had another idea. "I have a question. Why do you have those corrals out there? They look like they are supposed to be for pigs, but I don't see any."

Don Tacho looked at me and replied, half laughing, half serious, "No, we don't have any pigs. We use the corral for our goats."

"But I don't see any goats. Where are they?"

He pointed to the far-away mountains. "Right now they're up there in the pasture, where some of my grandchildren are taking care of them. They are brought to the corral to sleep at night and to be milked in the morning. Each day they are returned to the mountain pasture."

I kept looking around for other things I might help with. I had seen a mule tied under a tree in the back yard, and I had seen a carriage sitting under a canopy made of branches. "I wonder what they are using this for? Maybe to carry firewood from the mountains to their homes," I thought.

A Salvadoran's Journey

I paused long enough in my questioning so that Roberto had a chance to say something. "I would like to work with Ricardo in the morning."

"Glad to have you," the sheriff said. "Nice meeting you people. See you tomorrow morning."

After the sheriff left to return home, Don Tacho's wife, Doña Lupe, excused herself to prepare lunch. We talked a little more with Sylvester and his father. Actually, we mostly listened as Don Tacho is the kind of person who liked to talk. You had to be quick and fast to break into one of his conversations.

The next morning we were up early. As we left I saw some people milking the goats. It made me think back to when I was a little boy milking cows for my grandmother. But I was just as eager to help with harvesting. Roberto Lobo and I joined a crew of eight other men and worked from 8 a.m. to 2 p.m.

The stalks of seeds were waist high. We stood between the rows, bent over, and grabbed a bunch of stalks in each hand. Then we pulled them up by the roots, shook the dirt off, and bundled them. These bundles we stacked standing up like corn shocks, forming loose, teepee-like structures so they could dry. We worked for three days harvesting sesame seeds. I had seen sesame seeds being harvested in El Salvador, but this is the first time I had done this work myself.

At this point the seed pouches attached to the stalks were closed. We learned that after drying for two or three weeks, these little pouches would open and the seeds could be separated from the pouches. I didn't participate in this part, but I learned how it was done. A worker would grab a handful of stalks and walk over to a plastic sheet spread on the ground nearby. With one hand they would lightly spank

145

the upside down bundles with two-foot-long sticks so that the seeds fell onto the plastic tarp.

Soon after Roberto and I started harvesting sesame seeds, Sr. Vegas got Bartolo a job in the city of Los Mochis as a tailor. He went to live there, and sometimes we didn't even see him on the weekends. The boys spent their days with Sylvester's children, while Roberto and I moved on to picking cotton.

In the mornings, Doña Lupe rose at 5 a.m. When I heard her making noise in the kitchen, I would go to the kitchen, say good morning and get a metal pail to milk the goats. I already knew how to milk cows, and, after watching one day, I now knew how to milk goats. I enjoyed milking them. This was not only the beginning of my day, but the highlight of it. I liked being in the middle of all the animals.

Each day Doña Lupe made coffee for me to drink while I milked the goats. She would say, "The coffee is boiling hot. Cool it off a little with some goat milk." It always tasted good early in the morning like the milk from my grandmother's cows.

To milk goats, I didn't use a piece of rope like I had used to milk cows in El Salvador. Instead, I held the pail in my left hand, approaching the goat from her left side and facing forward. I bent down quickly, grabbing her left leg with my right hand, so she stood on three legs. I tucked her leg under my right knee, crouching down and closing my leg tightly, while shifting my weight to my left leg. Simultaneously, I slid the pail under the goat with my left hand. Now both my hands were free and I could milk the goat.

The goats were often too curious for their own good. By the time I had finished milking one goat, there were a bunch of goats walking around me, so I didn't have to stand up. I'd just grab the back leg of the goat closest to me, let go of the first goat, and move the pail under the second goat. With 150 goats in a small corral, it was easy to continue doing this until they were all milked.

By the time Doña Lupe's grandchildren joined me at 6 a.m., I was almost half finished. I had already collected the milk in large milk cans. I had to milk 20 goats to fill a pail. With the grandchildren's help finishing up, I could answer Doña Lupe's call to breakfast.

Doña Lupe was impressed that I could milk 75 goats in a little over an hour. Though others in this household were faster than I was, I certainly held my own. It was nice to be appreciated by the lady of the house, who was doing so much for us. I was happy being able to do something I liked and contribute to the household.

Roberto and I ate breakfast together. He was not so happy. For one thing, he was unhappy about Bartolo. Roberto had left El Salvador with Bartolo, who was his friend. Since Bartolo had gone to work in the city, Roberto felt abandoned. Roberto and I were just acquaintances and we came from different places. He lived in a village just outside San Luis de la Reina. We never had heart-to-heart conversations because we didn't have any shared experiences or memories. He never said he was unhappy, but I knew he was particularly disappointed on the weekends when Bartolo stayed in the city and didn't come to visit us.

The other thing Roberto was unhappy about was money. He was trying to save money, but he had to spend half of what he made picking cotton on lunch every day, buying tacos from the truck that came to the field each day at lunchtime. Doña Lupe wanted to make us lunch every morning, but we didn't want to make any more work for

BREAKING HOME TIES

her than she already had, so we only carried water. I ate fewer tacos than Roberto, and I picked more cotton, so I was saving more money then he was.

It was understandable that Roberto was hungry. Picking cotton was hard work. Every morning when we got to the field on the truck that picked up the laborers, we were handed cloth bags that looked like 10-foot-long pillowcases. These we strapped around our waists so the bags hung between our legs. Bending over slightly, we picked the cotton with both hands. When both hands were full, I tossed the cotton balls into the bag. One learned to grab the balls carefully and quickly to not get pricked by the thorny pod holding the cotton.

When each bag was full, we slung them over our shoulders and carried them to a clearing where the owners weighed our bags, recording the weight on a slip of paper. Then we emptied the bags onto a cart and went back to pick some more. When we had a few slips, we'd take them to the foreman and cash them in. If it was about noon, we'd buy tacos and pop. Around three o'clock we all quit and get into the truck for the ride back to San Ignacio.

After work we went with the young boys from the Vegas family and our three boys to the soccer field where we scrimmaged together with other Mexican men my age. Roberto just watched. There were enough players for two adult teams. All the kids played behind the goal post while I played with the men. Afterwards, the others sometimes gathered around me, saying they wanted to hear me talk so they could listen to my accent. Sometimes I would just have them gather around and I could listen to their accent. To me their rising and falling voices were like singing.

I was content with my life in Mexico. I had many soccer buddies, a paying job, and a good family to live with. I felt safe and productive. I couldn't remember the last time I had felt this way. At Doña Carmen's, the work was harder, lasted all the daylight hours, and I had no time for myself or for recreation. I would have been satisfied to stay in Mexico and work until I could return to El Salvador.

14

My Responsibility Deepens

My fantasy of staying with the Vegas family for a while longer, then returning to El Salvador didn't last long. Things began to move forward one day about three months after we had arrived in the village. One afternoon Roberto and I jumped down from the work truck and looked up to see Henrique and Camillo. What a surprise!

We had last met three months earlier when we were all in Colima. Christmas Eve at Doña Carmen's had been the time before that I had seen my paisanos, my countrymen.

At that time we had told Henrique and Camillo that we were headed for Los Mochis. I had figured that by this time they would have been much further on their way north than we were, or that they had already passed Los Mochis without stopping.

Henrique and Camillo were talking to Don Tacho and Doña Lupe. After they finished, I went up to the Vegases and vouched for my friends.

"I know these two guys," I said.

"Okay, everything is all right. You are friends of Ricardo's," Don Tacho said, " and you can stay here. We have a big place."

It turned out that Camillo and Henrique had stayed in Colima for three months continuing to work in construction. I remembered that after delivering produce for a while Natan had gotten a good job in Colima delivering oxygen tanks to hospitals and homes. Because

BREAKING HOME TIES

he had learned his way around Colima and the surrounding neighborhoods and because Natan had earned the trust of his boss, he was able to make thousands of pesos a day. I was a bit envious, as I was making only 300 a day.

All four of them had left Colima at the same time. Though Conce and Natan, with their greater earnings, were able to buy train tickets from Guadalajara all the way to Mexicali, Henrique and Camillo could only afford to buy tickets as far as Los Mochis, where they caught the bus to San Ignacio.

At the sight of my friends from San Luis, Roberto perked up a little. Although he had lived outside of San Luis in the countryside, he had known Henrique and Camillo. I was feeling sort of like the old man in the group, as Henrique and Camillo were near the same age, about ten years younger than I was, while Roberto was five years younger.

Later that afternoon, we all went together to the soccer field and played for a while. On our way back, Camillo asked, "Where's Bartolo?"

"He's got a job in Los Mochis. Sometimes he comes to spend the weekend with us, but he didn't come last weekend, so I am almost sure he will be coming here this weekend." I decided I didn't need at this time to share my worries about Bartolo with them.

Camillo and Henrique asked me, "What are you doing for money?"

"Roberto and I are picking cotton right now. Here it is easy to find a job. Do you want to work? I think you could start tomorrow."

"Of course! We don't want to be here doing nothing. Besides, we need to make some money to continue our trip north."

A Salvadoran's Journey

"Come to the field with us. Anybody can work." We were all glad, as now we were a pretty big group: four Salvadorans—Roberto, Henrique, Camillo, and myself—along with two teenage sons of the Vegas family plus a man who was a neighbor of the Vegases who was my age and his 18-year-old brother. The eight of us picked cotton and talked all day, which made the days, seem short.

We Salvadorans had numerous questions for Faustino, the neighbor who was my age, because we had learned that he had worked in the United States.

"What kind of job do you do in the U.S. that you can do for a few months and then return to Mexico?"

"I go up to Fresno to pick fruit," he said. "When the season is over, I come back. I think I have crossed the border at least a hundred times. I have only been caught once by the border patrol. If you all want to go with me, you need to be ready to leave in a few weeks."

I was startled. When I had first met Faustino I wondered it he was mentally retarded. He was always smiling. Smiling when he stood with the chickens. Smiling when he was standing next to the donkey. When he wanted to talk to someone, he moved very close and whispered. Sometimes I saw him talking to himself or talking to animals.

"By the end of this month I hope to have enough money saved up to take a train to Mexicali," said Faustino. "I have a cousin who lives there. If you come, we can all stay with him for a few days, cross the border, and then go up to Los Angeles. Anybody who wants to come with me can come. I am not a *coyote*. I am not charging any money to anybody for leading him to the U.S. What you have to do is follow my steps. You can keep me company. I just don't want to cross alone."

BREAKING HOME TIES

That evening before we fell asleep, I talked with Roberto, Camillo and Henrique. I told them that if Faustino hadn't saved enough money, it was our job to make it possible for him to make the trip so that we could go with him. We should give him enough money on the last day of work to make the amount he needed. The boys could make the connections to be with their parents in the United States. As we talked we grew anxious and eager to tell the good news to Bartolo, who was supposed to arrive on Saturday at noon.

On Saturday, as soon as I spotted Bartolo walking toward the house, I knew he had been drinking again. I realized that we were in a very awkward position now. I knew that once he started drinking he wouldn't stop for two or three months.

By the time Bartolo had stumbled and staggered his way the remaining blocks, everyone came outside to meet him. Roberto glanced over at me and then back to Bartolo.

I broke the silence. "Well, Bartolo, we've been making plans to continue the trip. You better get yourself sober because we are not going to be traveling with you if you are drunk." Then I said, "Why didn't you come last weekend? We missed you."

Bartolo told us that he had gone out the Friday night before with some new friends and that's when he started drinking beer.

"So didn't you go to work this past week?"

Bartolo looked down at the ground. "I went to work on Monday, but my boss told me not to come back. He said he didn't need anybody drunk working there."

A Salvadoran's Journey

I was embarrassed for my cousin and said, "You got that job because Don Tacho and Doña Lupe recommended you. Now you need to go and apologize to them."

Bartolo refused, so I went to Doña Lupe to apologize for him. I explained that he was not working in Los Mochis anymore because he had been drinking and that I felt I was going to have to be his mother and father because he was acting like a child.

"You don't have to apologize to me," she said. "It is not your fault. There are people like Bartolo here, too. That's not something new for me. The only thing is, he was supposed to be responsible for the children. Now you are stuck caring for the boys and for him."

"I hope he stops soon," I said, "because if he doesn't stop, I will call his sister."

It was the beginning of the month and we planned on leaving in three weeks, as we figured it would take that long to make the additional money to help Faustino, so I told Bartolo he had eight days to get sober, until the following Saturday.

But at the end of the eight days Bartolo was still drinking. Sometimes we had to give him money to stop him from going to people's houses and begging for money to drink. I gave him more money than the others did because I didn't want to be embarrassed that my cousin was asking for money from strangers. I decided to wait another week, though, just in case he could somehow quit.

On the second Saturday I went with Roberto to the nearby town of Ruiz Cortinas and made a collect call to Bartolo's sister, Bella, who was living in the U.S. She said she would send him some money so he could return to Honduras. Then Bella and I had a discussion about what should be done about the kids if Bartolo went back, and she told me that I would be in charge of them!

Bella shared a house with the boys' mother and father. Leon, the boys' father, got on the phone to talk with me. He asked me to bring the boys to Mexicali and gave me a name and address of someone there. Leon told me that a friend there would take the children over the border and that he and his wife would reimburse me for my expenses getting their boys to them in the US.

I agreed and said I would do my best, telling Leon that we were planning to leave in about two weeks.

I told Roberto that Bella had said that Bartolo should go back home.

"When we started out, I had a feeling Bartolo would spoil the trip," Roberto said. He paused. "Bartolo was going north because he wanted to join relatives there, and I was going north because I am Bartolo's friend. If Bartolo doesn't continue the trip north, I don't want to go either."

On our way back home I thought about the situation I was now in. When Henrique and Camillo had arrived, I had been optimistic that things would turn out positively. Together, I knew we could handle anything that came up. Then, after meeting Faustino and making plans to travel north with him, I had been even more confident about getting to the border to deliver the children. But when I saw Bartolo drunk, all these good, confident feelings had evaporated. Now, after talking with his sister, Bella, I felt that I had been saddled with a heavy responsibility that I was not prepared for.

When we got back home I explained the situation to the boys. The kids seemed to be excited and ready to continue the journey, except for Juanito, who was probably thinking about getting motion sick on the bus or train. They were happy during their time in Mexico, though they missed their parents in the US and their other relatives in El Savador and knew they soon would be going to another strange place.

When I said I was not anxious to go to the United States, the niños reminded me that they were anxious to see their parents. This resulted in feeling pulled in two directions: a desire to see the niños safely to the United States tugging against my own desires, which were being pushed further and further away.

In addition, what I had heard about the U.S. from other people sounded pretty negative. I had mixed thoughts about the US politically and the reality of returning to El Salvador seemed to be out of reach. Though I was impressed with what Faustino had told us, we learned that Sylvester Vegas had worked for three years in the U.S. and now he was back in Mexico. We had lots of time to listen to him talk about the U.S. because we were helping him work on his new house on the weekends.

"It is true that in the U.S. one is paid well," he said, "but they make you work hard for what you are paid and the apartments and food are expensive." It turned out that during the time he worked there he was able to save enough money so that now he could finish his house, so I thought he must have been paid fairly well.

In the middle of the week Roberto and Bartolo went to Ruiz Cortinas to pick up the money Bella had wired. They left for Honduras that weekend.

The boys were sad when Bartolo left, and in looking back now, I know that this was a turning point for me. Up to this time I had felt mostly as if I was on a big adventure. I had been thinking about staying right where I was. I knew I could have been happy there. The people knew I was a

BREAKING HOME TIES

fleeing Salvadoran and had sympathy for me. But now things had changed. The niños and I had been together about four months, and I felt closer to them, more like a parent. And like any parent, I felt a deep responsibility to see that they were safely on their way to their own parents' home.

Although I knew I had taken on a bigger responsibility, I decided that I could handle it since I was only going to drop the boys in Mexicali, not take them across the border into the U.S. I figured that if I did somehow end up getting into the U.S. I'd get arrested and deported from there. If that happened, I decided I would not try to come north again. So I let nature take its course...

15

Leaving Mexico

The Saturday night after my cousin Bartolo and Roberto Lobo left, we said goodbye to the Vegas family and our other new friends. One moment I especially treasure was when I said goodbye to Doña Lupe. She told me that they liked me as if I was part of the family. "All of my sons have gone to work in the north and not one has said that they wanted to live in the United States. So it's okay if you want to go and try to survive over there, but if one day you get deported or you don't want to live in the north, you don't have to go back to the situation in El Salvador. Think of this as your second home. You can come back to us."

It seemed like just a moment ago my grandmother had said, "If you don't like the new place that you are going to, know that you can always come back home anytime." I thanked Doña Lupe and gave her a hug. I told her that if one day I did not like living where I was, I would come back.

A dozen of us started walking to the train station, and more people joined the group. We must have looked like we were marching on a strike at the train station, some of us smiling and joking, others talking and laughing.

At 7 p.m. we boarded the train, *El Burrito*. Besides the three kids, and myself there were Camillo and Henrique, Faustino and his brother, plus Armando and Uriel, members of the Vegas family. This train didn't have any first- or second-class cars. Some cars didn't have windows, though all the cars were in the same class. Most of the people who traveled on this train went from station to station. It was a very slow train, which is why it was called "the little donkey."

We didn't have any problem with immigration because no one would believe there would be anyone on that train trying to go north. Normally, if one wanted to travel from Los Mochis to Mexicali, one would take *La Bala*, a fast passenger train that just stopped in the main railroad stations. Immigration officers would get on the train and search everybody. Central Americans would bribe the Mexican authorities to stay on "the bullet." At the next station they had to pay again. As soon as the money was gone, that was it.

Our train was half the price of the other one, but it was tough. We traveled all that night, all the next day, and the next night. The temperature at night in the desert was very cold. During the day, it was about 105 to 110 degrees. We went through deserts where sand rushed through the windows of the train. Inside the train, though we had a lot of space, everything was dusty. We put handkerchiefs over our noses and mouths so we could keep from breathing sand into our lungs. Before we left, Doña Lupe had packed us enough food and water for the two-day trip. It was well wrapped, so we didn't eat much sand. We looked like banditos, and our faces and hair were full of dust. Our clothes were dirty and we looked so terrible we laughed at each other. But the kids were not having a good time. They spent their time lying on the floor underneath the seats trying to avoid the dust—and, of course, the Mexican immigration.

Seeing that we were arriving in Mexicali, Faustino told us that we were going to have to get off the train before it reached the station. As the train slowed down, we just followed him. He jumped and we jumped off after him.

When all of us were on the ground, he told us to divide into three groups. We kept some space between the groups, about 20 yards. I was with the two youngest boys. Camillo and Henrique and the oldest boy were together. The other guys stayed together.

We had jumped off the train in the outskirts south of Mexicali. Faustino directed us to head east around the town. After walking for about half an hour, we got to a place that looked like slums. The place where Faustino's cousin lived looked like a meson. It consisted of small rooms made of concrete blocks built around a central area. That's where the outhouse facilities were also. I thought of Victor's escape in the meson in San Miguel.

This 35-year-old woman, Cristina, and her husband and children received all of us heartily. She welcomed us and asked if we were hungry. Faustino did not give her the falsely polite Salvadoran answer, "Yes, cousin, we're all very hungry."

Cristina went out and came back with beans, rice, and tortillas ready to eat. It was a great feast for all of us. Everybody thanked her for the dinner, and then I asked her about the address I had been given of the person who was going to take care of the three boys. I wanted to go the following day to find this person. Cristina knew where the place was as soon as she saw the address. She wrote on a piece of paper which buses I needed to catch to get there.

We went to bed rather early. Though we slept under the roof overhang outside in the courtyard without walls around us, I felt safe and comfortable. The niños slept in the middle of us. I fell asleep that night thinking about the young charges that I was going to say goodbye to the next day. In one way I was glad I was going to have less responsibility, but I knew I was going to miss them. This "adventure" was not only hard on children, it was difficult for us adults, too. I had never minded the responsibility of the children, and now I was glad that the boys were going to be with people who would care for them.

All of us got up at about 6 a.m. the next day. I told the boys where I was going and that I was not taking them with me because it was too risky, as we were close to the border and there were many authorities around.

I went to the address Cristina had given me, arriving at about seven. I knocked on the door. After knocking for a long time, a neighbor next door opened his door.

"If you're looking for Samuel, he's not home," the neighbor said. "He left eight days ago for New York. His daughter is sick and I don't think he'll be back for another week. I'm keeping an eye on his apartment."

"Thank you very much for your information," I said. "Can you do me a favor? In case Samuel comes back sooner, I would like to leave my name and address along with the name of the person who recommended that I contact him." I wrote this down on a piece of paper and gave it to the neighbor.

I took the bus back. I told the boys and my friends that I hadn't found Samuel and I didn't believe that I was going to, and that we had no other plan.

I talked with Faustino's relatives and told them that I had very little money. I decided to give all of my money to Cristina. That way she could continue to feed the niños. In the meantime, I called Leon collect to see if he had someone else who could be in charge taking his sons to Los Angeles.

A Salvadoran's Journey

It took Leon three days to find someone else to take the boys across the border. It was an older couple who said they'd take the kids and pass them as though they were their own children. Leon said that they had agreed to give me money for my expenses when I gave them the kids, and that he would later pay back this couple.

When the couple arrived, it was noon. I had sent the kids with Camillo and Henrique to a place about 12 yards away to a small grove on the outskirts of town. I introduced myself to the couple and told them that the father of the kids had told me I was supposed to receive $20 U.S. from them when I delivered the children.

The man said, "I didn't make any deals with the children's father to give you any money."

I had spent the last two days without eating, just drinking water in the park. I had turned over all my money to Christina to feed the children. That morning I had blurry vision. I couldn't see clearly, and I was shaking.

"If that is the case, you are not taking the kids. If I don't get the money, I am not supposed to turn the boys over to you."

When the man saw that I was serious, he said, "Okay, I will give you the $20. Where are the niños?"

"Hand me the $20 and they will be in front of you in three seconds," I told him.

He gave me the $20 and I whistled. The boys came out of the bushes. I introduced them to the man and his wife and told the boys that this couple was going to take care of them.

"Pay attention and obey everything that they tell you to do and, God willing, I'll see you in the U.S."

The couple knew where to take the kids in Los Angeles. I didn't know if I'd actually see them again, but I didn't

BREAKING HOME TIES

want to alarm the boys. I kept my fears to myself. When the niños were safely with the coyotes, it was a big relief to be on my own. Going from Mexico across the U.S. border was a dangerous adventure. My "job" was really finished because the kids were safe. Now whatever was going to happen was only going to happen to me myself.

I said goodbye to the boys. We Salvadoran and Mexican men gathered together and Faustino said, "We will be taking a bus from here to a town called Algodones."

Late that afternoon the seven of us each walked individually to the bus terminal and got on the bus. We didn't sit together, but sat close enough to keep an eye on each other so we could all see what was going on. Everything on the bus was calm. We saw the first edges of Algodones so we got off the bus. It was already dark as I stepped off the bus and noticed that it had been raining.

Faustino said, "You have to follow me and take the same steps I'm taking."

I was thinking that the authorities might easily be alerted to us. Faustino was concerned, and so was I.

I thought, "We are already here. We are not going to go back." We started following Faustino, but he soon stopped, hiding in the brush. In front of us was a bridge no more than 4 feet wide and about 30 to 40 yards long crossing an irrigation ditch.

Faustino passed the word, "We can't cross this now." He pointed to the other side of the channel. We were on the Mexican side, and on the other side, some distance away, was a van and a small group of people. "That's Immigration," Faustino said.

We moved even closer, but we had the water between the United States and ourselves.

A Salvadoran's Journey

After about 40 to 45 minutes, we heard the van start. Immigration was using flashlights to see and was driving without lights. After they left we waited about four long minutes. Then Faustino stood up and whispered loudly, "Let's go."

It was about nine o'clock when we started running toward the footbridge. I was afraid, but we crossed it quickly.

Now we were in the United States, but Faustino told us we had a long way to go to be safe. We continued running behind him. Most of the time we stayed way off to the side of the road, but when we had to cross any road, we turned around and ran across backwards, though continuing to move farther away from the bridge as fast as we could.

Suddenly we heard dogs barking from about two or three blocks away.

"Those are trained dogs from the border patrol," Faustino said. "I'm afraid of those dogs, not Immigration."

After an hour and a half running, I fell behind. I remember that we had talked before and decided that we were not going to wait for anybody if anybody got lost. I was very tired and thirsty, and, bending down on the side of a little ditch, drank some water, and then got up and continued running. I spent 10 minutes sprinting as fast as I could. When I got to the top of a small hill I could see far in the distance the reflections of the city lights shining over the whole sky. I stopped for a couple of seconds, and looked around in the near distance. It was dark and I couldn't see very much. I started running down towards a big light in front of me. This was the direction we had been running, so I assumed the guys were ahead of me somewhere. A half minute later I recognized Henrique's voice yelling, "Ri-carrrrr-dooo!"

BREAKING HOME TIES

I heard this loud and clear from about half a block away. I answered back, "I'm on my way!"

Soon I caught up to everybody. I had been separated from the group for no more than ten minutes, but it was very unnerving.

We continued running until we got to the railroad tracks. When we got to a section of tracks that was elevated over the low, flat land, we turned to our right and walked toward the bright lights of the city, which Faustino told us was Yuma, Arizona. By now it was about midnight.

The tracks ran east west between Los Angeles and Yuma. We followed them towards Yuma. Soon we reached a small railroad trestle with water running in a channel under the small bridge. We all stopped and bent down to drink. Then we got up, walked along the bank of the channel and crossed to the other side, where we continued running with the tracks on our right. We were wet, not from the water, but from our own sweat. To our left and ahead of us was a sort of arboretum of tall bushes and a few trees.

Faustino said, "Let's rest here for a moment and, hopefully, with good luck, a train will pass by soon."

We hid there for an hour or an hour and a half before we heard a train leaving the station. We could hear the steam whistle blow. At that moment, I started stretching my legs, which were tired from the earlier running. They were a little cramped and the closer the train got the more my legs trembled. Faustino called us together and told us, "I will give the signal. When I start moving, then you can start moving."

By the time Faustino finished talking, the train was very close. We let the first cars pass. After 15 or 20 cars, Faustino signaled and started running up the grade. By the time all of us were up the grade, the cars were speeding by.

166

A Salvadoran's Journey

We could feel the wind from the train. I figured that I couldn't get on the train at this speed, and I looked at all the other faces.

Camillo, who was the last one up the grade, didn't look, but tried to grab one of the ladders of the train and was sent flying down like a speck on a windshield. I ran to see how he was. Everyone followed me and went to help him. Thank God, he was not hurt badly, but he had scratches all over the left side of his face and arm and bruises from the fall. By this time, the train was gone, and it was about 1 or 2 a.m.

We walked back to the arboretum. We talked softly amongst ourselves and agreed to go closer to the train station, closer to the city of Yuma. We walked about four or five blocks and waited in another arboretum until 4:30 or 5:00 when we saw the sun starting to rise.

By the light of day, we looked around for a place to hide until the next train passed by. We remembered that when we crossed under the trestle opposite us on the other side of the tracks was a cotton field. We crossed the muddy banks of the tracks backwards and got into the cotton field. We moved to the center of the field where the cotton plants were about two feet tall. The plants were full of dark, green leaves and cotton balls.

We lay down in a small ditch between the rows of cotton. The leaves on our right covered half of our bodies and the ones on the left covered our other side. Whenever we wanted to see what was going on, we made a little hole and slowly raised our heads up through the leaves. Mostly, we saw pesticide-spraying planes and U.S. helicopters.

By noon it was very hot and we were hungry and thirsty. We kept eating cottonseeds. We spent the whole day until dusk lying on our backs or sides in this cotton

BREAKING HOME TIES

field. When it started to get dark, we began crawling on our knees and elbows toward the water channel we had crossed the night before. Again we drank as much water as we could hold. After we had our fill, we went back to the small windbreak to wait for a train.

After about 20 minutes of hiding and waiting, we heard the train whistle. In our excitement, we started again. The same instructions as last night: We were going to run after Faustino. After he jumped on the train, we were going to follow him. When I saw the train, my heart started beating faster. After the engine passed us, I counted about a dozen more cars. Faustino jumped and said, "Let's go!"

We followed him up the gravel grade. By the time I got up to the top of the grade, I saw that he was climbing onto the train from where he had jumped. At that moment I saw his brother jump and grab one of the ladders and get on the train, too. Next was Camillo, then Henrique. When I saw they were up and that the train was going faster, I knew it was not going to get any better. I saw the faces of Uriel and Armando and I started running with the train because I didn't see any ladder or any part of the train that I could grab with my hands and hold. I tried to jump up onto a flatbed car and I only could grab on with my elbows. I just squeezed down with my elbows and held my body up as the train continued gathering speed. There was nothing for my hands to grasp. I could feel the wind of the wheels sucking and trying to pull my legs toward them. I turned my head and saw Armando and Uriel a block away just standing there and looking at the train speeding by.

I had hung there for about two blocks when I saw lights flashing on to the side of the train. People stood on the grade next to a white car parked below the grade. As my car passed by, they shone their flashlights on me. When a man tried to grab me, I kicked out with my right leg on his chest and knocked him down the grade. I sort of gave up at this moment. Then I heard Henrique say, "Hold on. I'm on my way to help you."

Henrique came out from under the semi-truck container sitting on his platform car and moved onto my car. He walked under the semi on my car, sat with his back against one of the tires, and grabbed one of my arms. That way I had something to hold on to as I swung one leg up. Then he pulled me a little more and my chest was on top of the platform and then my other leg was up. Henrique had really saved my life.

When I got up onto the platform I lay on my back wet with sweat, though I was on the windy side of the train. I lay there shaking. After I relaxed for a moment, Henrique and I went to find the others. They were about three cars in front of us. When we got there, someone noticed that the backs of my arms didn't have any skin on them and they were both bleeding.

"My scraped arms are nothing compared to what I've just been through," I said.

Because I was the last one to get on the train, they asked me about Uriel and Armando.

"I saw them standing up on the grade," I told them, "and they looked as if they were not going to jump onto the train."

I never knew what happened to them after I last saw them standing there.

The five of us—Faustino and his brother and Camillo, Henrique, and I—hoped and prayed that the train would not make any stops. We didn't want to be caught by Immigration on our way to Los Angeles. Luck was on our side because at about 11:30 p.m. Faustino said, "We are getting into L.A."

When the train slowed down to about 5 or 10 miles an hour in downtown Los Angeles, Faustino said, "Let's get off here."

The train was going so slowly that we just about walked off. When I got off and started walking, I felt the pain of cramps in my legs. I saw the rest of the guys limping too. Then I remembered how we had run the night before and the night before that. Other worries had kept me from thinking about this as we crossed the border.

Faustino told us, "We are now in the City of Angels." We walked for about four blocks. I asked them to wait for me. I went behind a big trashcan and took off one of my shirts, the dirty one, and put it in the trash along with one of my pairs of pants and put them in the trash. When I returned everybody looked at me and smiled. I invited them for coffee and donuts with part of the $20 I had gotten from the couple that had taken the boys.

After we had finished, I walked to a public phone and called one of my primos. "He's working right now. Call him after 8 a.m. tomorrow," his brother-in-law answered.

So, in pairs, we wandered around the rest of the night until morning.

I called again after 8 a.m. and nobody answered. I continued calling every half-hour. We continued walking so we wouldn't be in one spot too long; we were afraid the authorities would ask us what we were doing.

At about 4 o'clock in the afternoon my cousin finally picked up the phone.

"I'm here in downtown L.A," I said. "Can you give me some shelter for a few days?"

"Sure," he said. "That's no problem. Where are you?"

A Salvadoran's Journey

I was on a corner and I gave him the names of the streets at the intersection. It must have been close to where he lived because it was only about 10 minutes before he arrived.

When my cousin got to where the five of us were, I told the guys, "Wait for me here. I want to talk to him for a minute."

I approached my cousin, shook hands, and gave him a hug.

"Can you help us?" I said. "We came last night and my friends don't know anybody here, and you're the only person I know here in Los Angeles."

"No problem," he said. "Let's get into the car and go to my place."

My cousin fed us as soon as we got to his apartment. He gave us towels and told us to take a shower because we smelled. Then he gave some of his small, outgrown clothing to Faustino and his brother. There was no way he could have given me anything that would fit me because he weighed about 200 pounds and I probably weighed less than 120. He asked me, "Rica, why do you look cleaner than the other guys?"

"I wore double pants and double shirts when I crossed," I said.

I called Leon and asked him to buy me a ticket for the same flight the boys were on. I breathed a little easier now, as I knew I'd see the niños again.

My cousin took Faustino and his brother to the train station the next day and bought them one-way tickets to Fresno.

Now it was just Henrique, Camillo, and I. Henrique and Camillo decided to stay with my cousin and work in Los Angeles for a while.

BREAKING HOME TIES

Two days later my cousin took me to the L.A. airport where we met up with the kids. Now I was nervous because I realized I was going to be in the air and I had never flown before. The three boys had never flown before either. I tried to look very calm and confident in front of them. My cousin walked us to the gate and we all said goodbye as we boarded the plane.

On the plane, the boys sat very close to me. I sat next to a window and enjoyed the view outside. Basilio and Saul looked relaxed, and Juanito, who had thrown up on buses, was not having any difficulties either, a relief to me.

The stewardess came by with her cart and asked the boys what kind of soda they wanted. The boys looked surprised and just stared at her face. She picked up a Coke and a 7-Up, and the boys pointed to the cans they wanted, then looked at me as if to ask if it was all right. I nodded.

Next the stewardess went to serve a Mexican man in front of me. I heard her say something in English, but I didn't pay much attention to what she said because I hadn't heard English before so I couldn't understand what she said. I did pay attention to what the Mexican said to her.

When it was my turn and she talked to me, I still didn't know what she was saying. I looked at her and when I saw that she had finished talking, I repeated what the man in front of me had said, "Jack Daniels, please."

She gave me a little bottle of liquor, a can of soda, and a glass of ice. I had the drink, and then I had another two because I was getting along so easily with my expanded English vocabulary.

By the time we got to Washington State, I was smiling, happy, and a little high. We deplaned and the niños ran to their parents' arms.

A Salvadoran's Journey

And there was my own family: Bella and Oscar, Natan and Conce, and even Victor. I knew we could all depend on each other. Here I could be stable for a while and, maybe, realize my dreams.

Epilogue

It was December when I arrived in the United States. The first snow I ever saw was in the State of Washington. Oscar built a snow bear. We had great fun in the snow while we tried to find work. There were many Mexicans and Mexican-Americans working in rural Washington. As Salvadorans we knew we had to try and fit into this new culture. If we could pass as Mexicans, we were more likely to get a job and less likely to be deported. I, personally, did not hide the fact that I was a Salvadoran. I would have been happy to go home.

I wrote many letters home. I thanked the Vegas family and wrote Doña Carmen. My sister, Beatriz, told me the National Guard had killed Tony. They claimed it was by mistake. I have kept in touch with Tony's widow and have sent money when I could to her and my friend's two sons.

Not being able to get a job because I wasn't legal sent me into a deep depression. I did find work-picking fruit with other migrant workers and 'illegals.' I continued to write letters as I had a lot of time on my hands. When I was in this depression and heard about the heavy fighting in El Salvador, I was anxious to go home and fight with the muchachos in the mountains. At one time or another, we all had these feelings. Luckily we did not all have these feelings at the same time. We knew our lives were not in danger and our presence in the US gave peace of mind to our families in El Salvador.

BREAKING HOME TIES

I still did not have a regular job in 1982. I received a letter from Beatriz that devastated me. She wrote that my grandmother had died. "The funeral," she said, was two weeks ago." Two weeks ago! I could have gone to my grandmother's funeral. I could have been there for the nine day mourning period. I was furious. I couldn't forgive my sister. Beatriz explained, "I promised our grandmother before she died that I would not tell you, so that you wouldn't leave the United States and come back to El Salvador." My grandmother had taken comfort in her last days that I was safe.

I still enjoy fishing. Catching one fish at a time is something I never thought I'd have the patience for. It's quite enjoyable to wrap fishing line around a can and 'cast' the line, hook and bait into the lake. Then I fill the can with water and set it on the dock. When the can tips over, I know I've got a bite.

As I stated in the preface to my first book, our children and grandchildren want to know who we were... If any of these words help, I'm glad.

About the Author

J. Ricardo was the original pen name of Ricardo Pocasangre. Just before the book went to print he decided to put his own name on the book. It's been 20 years since this story took place, yet he still has fears. He wants to protect his family and friends, but realizes that taking ownership of his writing may serve as a model, an example to future generations of Salvadorans in the United States.

The book went through many titles; <u>El Salvador: Remembering and Leaving</u>, and <u>El Salvador: At Home and On the Road</u> were two. There's an inspiring irony about <u>BREAKING HOME TIES</u>. Ricardo, orphaned at 5, has been returning to his country since 1986 caring for orphans in El Salvador.

In 1998 Ricardo Pocasangre and his wife started a family project called **NESES, Niños Estudiando El Salvador** (Children Studying El Salvador -www. NESES.org). They rent a bus and take 25 kids plus the bus driver and the cobrador on a weeklong trip all over El Salvador. The children from the *hogar del niño* (place of the child) have a chance to study their country. They have visited museums, national parks, businesses, ancient ruins, repatriated communities, newspapers, UCA, the teleferico, the airport, the seaport, and the Assembly. The Pocasangres fund this project on their own and work with the Salvadoran Institute for the Protection of the Minor.

Before and after these trips Ricardo visits with the children, stays in touch with them after they have left the orphanage and sponsors some of these young people with high school and college tuition and room and board. His abuelita would have been proud that he hasn't broken his home ties.

177

Appendix A

MAPS

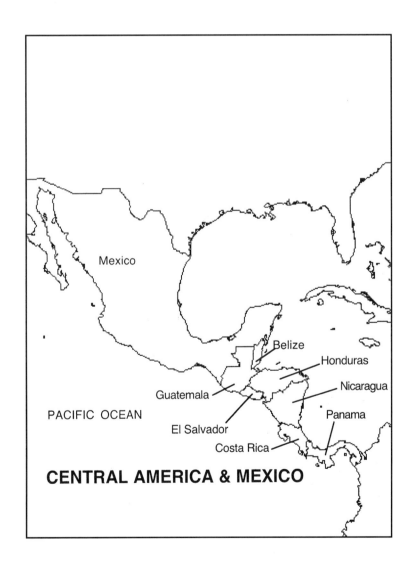

Mexico

PACIFIC OCEAN

Belize

Honduras

Nicaragua

Guatemala

El Salvador

Panama

Costa Rica

CENTRAL AMERICA & MEXICO

BREAKING HOME TIES

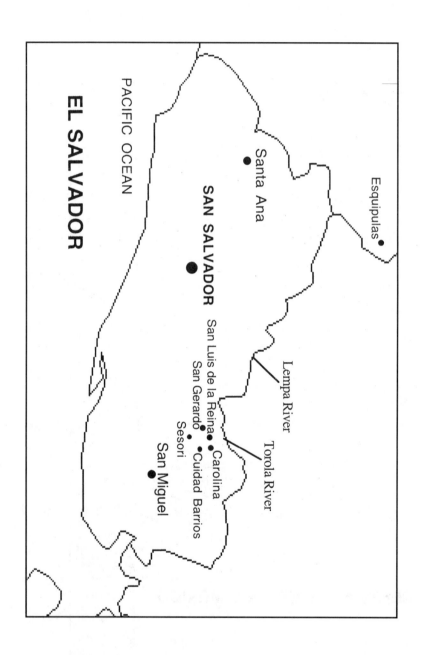

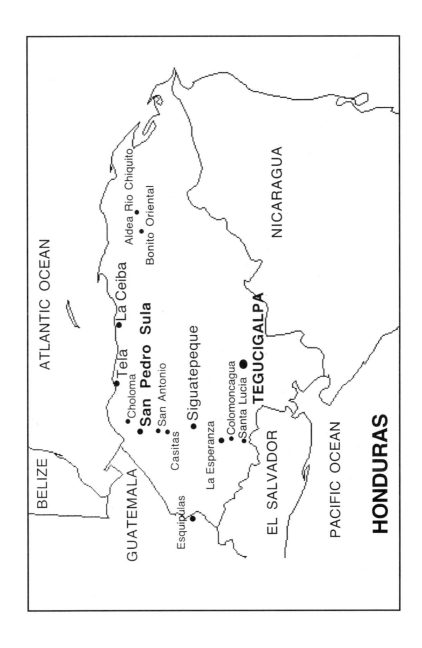

BREAKING HOME TIES

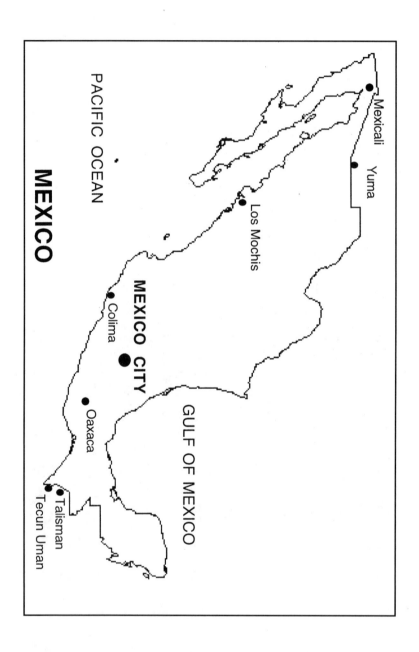

Appendix B

GLOSSARY

abuelita, grandmother

aserrador, a logger or lumberjack (sawyer)

atolé, a liquid pudding made with corn and milk

barra, a steel rod four feet long and two inches in diameter that resembles a crowbar

barrilete, an 8-foot, two-man saw

bendito, blessed

bolson, a cloth bag with a string shoulder handle

brazada, the length of a man's outstretched arms from fingertip to fingertip

calabazo, a gourd that is dried and used for carrying water

calandria, lark

campesinos, people who live in the countryside and farm other peoples' land

caracol, snail-shaped intersection

casa communal, a community center or community house

cejo 2 ft. stick, used to keep calves away when milking

chaparro, a type of moonshine

cobrador, an assistant to a bus driver, in charge of collecting fees and stowing luggage on top of the bus

colima, a meter-long machete

colon (colones), one colon = $.25 (in the 70's & 80's)

BREAKING HOME TIES

cordel, woven string bed frame
coyote, person who smuggles illegals into the US for $
cuajada, a type of homemade cheese
departamento, the equivalent of a state or province
dedos, informants, literally fingers
ejidos, small villages
espeton, a metal skewer
fianza, a deposit
frontera, border
futbol, soccer
garrobos, iguanas
Gracias a Dios, Thank God
guayavillas, a dwarf sort of guava that is very acidic
hornilla, outdoor, clay oven or barbecue
hospedaje, small roadside lodging
jefe, boss
lempira, one lempira = $.50 (in the 70's & 80's)
manzana, a field 50 brazadas square
matatas, handmade string bags
mayoristas, wholesalers
mentiroso, liar
mercado, market
muchacho, rebel fighter during the war, teenager
niños, boys, children
paisanos, countrymen
pelon, bald person
pension, rooms for rent
petate, a straw mattress
pezote, a small wild cat

A Salvadoran's Journey

primo, cousin

quetzales, Guatemalan, $ .35=1 US dollar

riachuelo, smaller than a river and bigger than a stream

sierra, a mountain range

tacos, soccer shoes

tamalitos, fresh corn tamales

tepezcuinte, paca, rabbit-like rodent

tia,tio, aunt,uncle

tiangue, livestock market

trabajador de caminos, road maintenance worker

trapiche, a hut where sugar cane is processed

trucha, a store that's an after-work gathering place for men

varones, men, males, guys

zancudo, a type of large, long-legged mosquito

Appendix C

SUGGESTED READINGS

Alvarado, Elvia. [Trans. and Ed. by Medea Benjamin]. *Don't Be Afraid, Gringo: A Honduran Woman Speaks from the Heart.* New York: Harper & Row, 1989.

Argueta, Manlio. [Trans. by Clark Hansen]. *Cuzcatlán: Where the Southern Sun Beats.* New York: Vintage Books/Random House, 1987.

Argueta, Manlio. [Trans. by Bill Brow]. *One Day of Life.* New York: Vintage Books/Random House, 1983.

Didion, Joan. *Salvador.* New York: Simon and Schuster, 1983.

Foley, Erin. *El Salvador.* New York, London, Sydney: Marshall Cavendish, 1995.

Gettleman, Marvin E., Patrick Lacefield, Louis Menashe, David Mermelstein, and Ronald Radosh, eds. *El Salvador: Central America in the New Cold War.* New York; Grove Press, Inc., 1981.

Kuffeld, Adam. [Photographs by, Intro by Arnoldo Ramos, Poetry by Manlio Argueta] *El Salvador.* New York, London; W.W. Norton & Co, 1990

BREAKING HOME TIES

Menjivar, Cecilia, *Fragmented Ties: Salvadoran Immigrant Networks in America*. Berkeley: University of California Press, 2000.

Morrison, Marion. *El Salvador*. Chicago: Children's Press, 2001. [Enchantment of the World, Second Series]

Merrill, Tim. L., ed. *Honduras: A Country Study*. Washington, D.C.: Federal Research Division, Library of Congress, December 1993.

Murray, Kevin with Tom Barry. *Inside El Salvador: The Essential Guide to its Politics, Economy, Society, and Environment*. Albuquerque, New Mexico: Resource Center Press, 1995.

Ricardo, J. *El Salvador: A Memory of Home*. Redmond, Washington: CentAm Publishing, 1991, 1993.

Rodriguez, Mario Menendez. *Voices from El Salvador*. [Trans. from the original Spanish edition, *El Salvador: Una Autentica Guerra Civil*] San Francisco: Solidarity Publications, 1983.

Targ, Harry R., and Marlene Targ Brill. *Honduras* Chicago: Childrens Press, 1995. [Part of Enchantment of the World series]

Vigil, José Ignacio López. [Abridged and translated by Mark Fried]. *Rebel Radio: The Story of El Salvador's Radio Venceremos*. Latin American Bureau/Curbstone Press, 1991.